FOCUSED

ANDREW NICHOLSON

FOCUSED

MY LIFE IN PICTURES

Andrew Nicholson

with Catherine Austen

Foreword by Captain Mark Phillips

RACING POST

Copyright © Andrew Nicholson and Catherine Austen 2014

The right of Andrew Nicholson and Catherine Austen to be identified
as the authors of this work has been asserted by them in accordance
with the Copyright, Designs and Patents Act 1988.

First published in Great Britain in 2014
By Racing Post Books, 27 Kingfisher Court, Hambridge Road,
Newbury, Berkshire RG14 5SJ

10 9 8 7 6 5 4 3 2 1

A catalogue record for this book is available from the British Library.

ISBN 978-1-909471-58-0

Cover designed by Jay Vincent
Designed and typeset by J. Schwartz & Co.

Printed and bound in the Czech Republic by Finidr

Every effort has been made to fulfil requirements with regard to copyright
material. The author and publisher will be glad to rectify any omissions at
the earliest opportunity.

www.racingpost.com/shop

CONTENTS

FOREWORD

By Captain Mark Phillips

I FIRST MET ANDREW in Auckland in 1984 after the Los Angeles Olympic Games. I had been invited along with other riders to compete in an invitational event on borrowed horses against the "home team". Watching Andrew there on the cross-country, I remember thinking: "That lad has talent."

Andrew has always been a very strong rider: lean, fit and with fantastic balance, all of which contributed to his "Mr Stickability" reputation. Coming out of the water at Badminton in 2014 on Nereo is the only time I can ever remember him actually falling off, while the moments he has survived, particularly on Mr Smiffy at Burghley in 2000, have become legendary in the sport.

Andrew has always had the ability to ride anything and, indeed, has ridden horses for me. On a difficult one, I would rate him one of the best riders of all time.

In his early days, Andrew was often outspoken and made his feelings very clear in the heat of the moment. Many officials would rather not have been the ones to give Andrew bad news!

I remember being technical delegate at Blenheim one year when he was interfered with by a tractor shuttle near the end of the cross-country course. As his blood pressure rose when I told him I could adjust his time, but not his 20 penalties, I really thought he was going to take a swing at me!

The Andrew of today is a very different person. His riding has improved, particularly on the flat and over the coloured poles, and if Andrew Nicholson says something today, you are a fool if you don't listen. His opinion is one of the most respected in the sport. Certainly when he's been acting as rider representative at events he has helped me on many occasions.

As a rider, Andrew now represents the whole package. He's very good with his owners, has established a great back-up team, has excellent attention to detail and gets the most out of the exceptional team of horses he has developed.

To be at the top of the sport at his age you need to keep super-fit and to keep riding good horses, which allows you to ride well. I take my hat off to him. I retired from eventing at the age of 40 after the 1988 Seoul Olympics. I can remember the relief when, in my last year, I was in the lorry park at Crookham with a bunch of novice horses to ride on a foul day and they announced over the tannoy that the event was cancelled!

Andrew has managed to retain his appetite for the sport; nobody rides more different and difficult horses in a day. At the same time, he's managed to retain his standards and hone his skills. Nobody begrudges him the world number one mantle; it is so deserved, and we all look forward to the next time he makes the art of crossing the country look so incredibly easy.

DEDICATION

For my mother, Heather, who taught me anything was possible in life –
you just had to work hard to achieve it.

ACKNOWLEDGEMENTS

None of my success would have happened without my brother John, who
made me get on the plane to England aged 18, and without the kindness and
support of the Powell family who took me in when I arrived. Finally, I would
like to thank every owner who has given me a horse to ride – good or bad!
Every one of them has contributed to my journey.

INTRODUCTION

By Andrew Nicholson

MY LIFE HAS CENTRED AROUND HORSES, and I thought the best way to illustrate this was to show you the pictures of them along the way. Anyone who knows me will also know I am not a big fan of reading books. Even as a child, I would choose the books with the best pictures as they were the ones that caught my attention.

I hope it is interesting to see some images from the early days, where I came from and how I worked my way to the top level of the sport. Perhaps it might show some younger riders today that you don't need to come from a wealthy background to make it to the top in this – or any other – sport. It's more about the work you put in, your self-discipline and dedication, and being prepared to push yourself outside your comfort zone and not be frightened to make mistakes along the way.

As you will see, it's not about winning every time. I have often learnt more from my mistakes and the bad days than those when it has all gone to plan. The experience has helped me take the next step up.

One thing that concerns me when I watch some of the very talented young riders today is that they are constantly being watched and instructed by someone. I think it is vital that as a rider you have the opportunity to think for yourself, and in doing so maybe make the occasional mistake. Often, things don't go to plan, and this is how you will develop the ability to react to such situations.

I am often asked what still motivates me to continue, and that's simple really: I motivate myself. I have never needed anyone to drive me and I am probably pretty stubborn and single-minded in this respect. The repetitive daily routine involved in training horses requires you to be self-motivated; the competitions are the easy bit. Underlying this drive has to be the constant challenge of finding and producing the young horses, and, hopefully turning them into winners. This I love.

My greatest weakness would be buying nice young horses. I prefer to buy them as three-year-olds so I can break them in myself and control all aspects of their training, and I am always planning ahead to ensure I will have a strong team at each level. There will always be some that aren't as talented as I had hoped, and others that will surprise me, but I normally know within a couple of days of breaking them in which ones have the brain and ability to make it.

I get the greatest pleasure when the young horses successfully take a step up to the next level. At the top end of the sport I am riding very good horses and the expectation is they will go well, but this isn't the case with the young ones. They can be winning one week, and have a disaster the next; you can't take anything for granted. When I win a major event on a horse I have broken in and started from scratch, the buzz and satisfaction it gives me is my incentive to carry on.

It has always been in my heart to be the best at what I do, and be number one in the world, but first and foremost I have to make a living. It was this basic necessity that started my involvement with horses, breaking in young thoroughbreds for trainers in New Zealand and then working as a farrier at the age of 15. I then progressed to earning money from training and selling horses, and finally from the prize-money. The financial principle is the same today.

While the sport has changed immeasurably since I started, most notably with the change to short-format competition after the Athens Olympics in 2004, my methods of training are very much the same. I was glad to get rid of the steeplechase and roads and tracks elements as the injuries caused by the steeplechase would inevitably shorten horses' careers and no one, least of all the spectators, really appreciated the pointless mileage you had done before you even started the cross-country.

However, I still have my horses just as fit for the short-format sport as they were for the long-format, if not fitter. Modern cross-country courses are intense jumping experiences, as the fences often have hard brush on top and square profiles. These make jumping a bigger physical effort, as horses jump very high and round over them. There are often clusters of obstacles on a course, which can be very tiring, and fewer "let-up" fences or galloping stretches compared to the old days.

The type of horse I have now is very different to the early part of my career. As has been well-documented, the rise in the standard of the dressage and showjumping phases has led to the need for good-moving and careful jumping horses, so the modern warmblood has become increasingly popular.

I would still choose to ride a thoroughbred, however, if I could find one that moved and jumped well enough. In general, they remain the elite athletes and are never stretched to their maximum physically in the overall effort of eventing. With that in mind I try to find horses with as much thoroughbred in their pedigree as I can.

As the format of the sport has changed, so have the events on offer. During my career, we have gone from having only two four-star events, both in Britain (Badminton and Burghley) to six world wide. When I first went to Pau in southern France it was only at two-star level and I was the first foreign rider who had ventured that far. Nowadays Pau and Luhmühlen are excellent four-star competitions alongside Badminton, Burghley, Kentucky and Adelaide.

That really makes the sport global. This has encouraged top-level sponsorship, such as for the FEI Classics series (which links the four-star events). This is so important if the sport is to get the consistent media exposure and essential television coverage which ultimately will deliver the level of prize-money the top riders deserve.

At the other end of the scale, there is a depressing trend as the prize-money at lower-level national events continues to decrease. I understand the economics more than most riders; both my wife Wiggy and I were heavily involved with the early days of what was then PERA – the Professional Event Riders Association, which was set up in the 1990s to try to achieve better standards of prize-money. What was a once-in-a-generation chance to put eventing on a proper commercial footing failed through mishandling, sadly. But there is no coordinated initiative evident from the governing bodies of eventing to halt the trend.

I can't help wondering whether some of those in charge don't have the core desire to see eventing and its participants make money. Sometimes necessity was the mother of invention, and the right people with the right attitude could change the outdated culture of opinion that is so often voiced behind the scenes in this country, where those riders – and there still aren't that many – who rely on making money from the sport for their livelihoods are seen as unsporting villains. Gone are the days where riders and owners were part of an old school club; it's tough to succeed, and you have to be focused.

THE MAN BEHIND THE LEGEND

By Catherine Austen

WHAT ARE THE CHARACTERISTICS OF SOMEONE who has spent 30 years at the top of an extreme sport? Physical strength and durability. Extraordinary mental toughness. Courage. The ability to overcome pain. Determination to succeed. Positivity. A never-ending desire to improve. The ability to focus entirely on achieving goals. An intensely competitive nature. And, of course, a great deal of talent in the first place.

If that extreme sport is eventing, where every facet of horsemanship is tested, we must add a perfect sense of timing, sensitivity, lightning-quick reactions, the indefinable quality of "feel", excellent organisational capabilities, adaptability, entrepreneurial skills – and the personal charisma to attract, and keep, owners.

All these Andrew Nicholson possesses. And he has something else besides: an inestimable amount of experience. His career has, so far, spanned almost every major competition between 1984 and 2014. He has almost certainly ridden more horses in more events that anyone else and learnt something from each one. At the age of 53, it is no exaggeration to say that he is riding better than he has ever done, and is reaping the rewards of three decades of relentlessly hard work.

Jenny Macarthur has been *The Times*' equestrian correspondent for the duration of Andrew's career. "He is the most instinctive rider I have come across," she says. "He is so light and balanced – you feel he is giving the horse every chance and making it as easy as possible for him."

Jenny remembers Andrew riding at his first Badminton in 1984. "He was fairly untutored, but you could not mistake his raw, natural style. Now his riding has been honed and polished into something much more sophisticated."

Andrew makes eventing look easy. So often first to go round the cross-country at the sport's biggest competitions, he flies round inside the time allowed and everyone heaves a sigh of relief. There is a great comfort and reassurance in watching him: the track is jumpable and all will be well.

This is sometimes false security. Just because Andrew can do something does not mean that other riders can too.

"I remember how he always used to be sent out first for the New Zealand team," continues Jenny Macarthur. "Mark Todd [team-mate since 1984] once said that their great team successes were due to Andrew's information – he was so brilliant at delivering feedback on a cross-country course."

By the 1990s, the New Zealand eventing team was conquering the world. Mark Todd had lit the touch-paper with his individual Olympic golds in 1984 and 1988; Blyth Tait, Olympic champion in 1996, continued banging the New Zealand drum by twice winning the world championship, in 1990 and 1998, while another team member, Vaughn Jefferis, took the title in 1994. Andrew, Blyth and Mark were the pillars that carried the team to world championship gold in 1990 and they dominated again in 1998. Although Olympic team gold eluded the trio, they won silver in 1992 and bronze in 1996 – and for good measure finished second in each of the "Open" European championships held in 1995 and 1997.

After something of a lull, New Zealand fought its way back into the medal table at the 2010 World Equestrian Games and the 2012 Olympics. This revival was spear-headed by Andrew as team Captainain, and backed up by Mark, who came out of retirement in 2008.

Andrew and Mark, who is five years older, may be among the senior members of the eventing fraternity now, but these tough-as-teak men with six decades of accumulated experience between them are harder than ever to beat. "I could see Andrew carrying on for another 15 years," says his friend and fellow competitor Oliver Townend.

Unlike some of his colleagues at the top of eventing, Andrew did not have family money to support him in a sport in which it is particularly hard even to make a decent living, let alone achieve a fraction of the wealth other top sportsmen accumulate. It takes exceptional strength of character to fly to the other side of the world and graft your way ceaselessly to success.

Jenny Macarthur comments: "Thirty years ago eventing had rather a 'cosy' image. Andrew has changed that. He is more like a true sportsman in his attitude – you can see how much it means to him, and the public could recognise that."

Andrew's ability on a horse is outstanding. Beanie Sturgis, an event rider acknowledged for her own natural talent, particularly across country, says: "He has amazing hands, and amazing balance. He just gallops along resting his hands lightly on his horse's neck in a rhythm and never moves on them or interferes."

Andrew would be the first to admit that, while riding cross-country came naturally to him, he has had to work hard at the dressage phase. "A bit of it was getting out of the mind-set of obtaining quick results with a horse in order to sell it. I could hold a horse in shape for a whole test – and that can still come in handy," he says with a flash of a grin.

For many years, Andrew's priority was achieving a profit on a horse. He bought them cheaply – mostly thoroughbreds off the New Zealand racetrack, often found by his older brother, John – and sold them once they had earned some decent results. He had to; he was building a business from scratch and had a family to support.

Gradually, he has improved the overall quality of the team of horses he competes, and now his Westwood Stables houses a string which is among the finest anywhere in the world. "I buy much nicer horses to start with now, and I pay good money for them," he says. "I can do that now, but if I had known, aged 25, I would have borrowed the money and paid for better horses. I was getting them as cheap as possible, usually by going to sales and buying a job lot. I worked on the theory that one of them would be good, two of them I would be able to make a quick profit on and a couple I would have to take a loss on – but it would be a small loss.

"Now a quick buck is less important, I can take my time with young horses. Buying them as three-year-olds means you can control everything they see and do. You can do things with them when the time is right, not because you have to. That's how horses stay sound. It's not because my horses now necessarily have better conformation; it's what they've done as youngsters. I regret the way I used some horses to get a swift turn-around, but at the time I had to make the numbers add up. First of all, you have to make a living. Then you can build on that, and now I'm in a position to take my time."

Andrew's wife Wiggy gives a fascinating insight into how he works with young horses.

"Quite a while ago I was in New Zealand looking for horses to buy and ended up at John Nicholson's farm," she says.

"Andrew was there, looking at a couple of thoroughbred horses off the track that John had found for him. John led out a three-year-old with its tack on, and Andrew stood and looked at it, while I wondered who was going to do what with it, in the field where we stood. Andrew then proceeded to hop on in his jeans and docksider shoes with no hat.

"A typical horse off the track, its head was in the sky and you could just about steer it. In three minutes Andrew had it trotting and cantering around on the bit, and after five minutes he started jumping. In ten minutes it was confidently clearing 1m 10cm, having never left the ground before.

"History doesn't relate whether the horse made the cut and got on a plane to the UK, but it was the process that amazed me. Everyone has witnessed Andrew's skills in public, riding in competition, but his unique ability to break and produce young horses goes on behind the scenes.

"He backs them in the stable and rides them first on the walker before trotting them down to the arena and off they go, and that's all in one day. I am not suggesting anyone else should or could try to emulate him, but it's quite something to watch, let alone to get on one only a week after he has started it and feel how rideable it is, having been taught all the aids clearly and been given the confidence to go where it is told."

Unusually, around half the horses currently in his yard come from Spain, bred either by former eventer Ramon Beca or his sister Ana. These gifted, clever and sharp horses are ideally suited to Andrew's own temperament and way of riding, and he finds working with them stimulating and rewarding.

Andrew is, he says, a person who has to learn things for himself. "It's part of my character. I learnt a lot about cross-country riding the hard way, by finding myself upside down on the floor with a horse on top of me. No one told me not to gallop to an upright gate – I learnt by doing it."

Annabel Scrimgeour has worked with Andrew for several years now, helping him school his horses on the flat. "I don't try to tell him what to do," she says. "He's a very good horseman who hasn't got to where he is without knowing a lot. But our strengths blend in well together: I make suggestions and tell him what the horses look like while he is doing something. He's not cocky about his ability, but he has confidence in his way of doing things."

Annabel continues: "He's very strong, physically and mentally. But it's not brute force – his horses adore him. He has a tremendous bond with them. He has a superb team of horses at the moment, but it is he who has made them brilliant. He is very good at accepting where their deficiencies lie and working around – and through – them. He knows when to push and when not to.

"And a lot of riders think they work very hard – and then they see what he does. I remember him arriving home at 9am after driving all night back from France, where he'd won the four-star at Pau on Nereo, and spending the rest of the day riding his three-year-olds."

There were five years between Andrew's first four-star (top level) triumph – at Burghley in 1995 – and his second, also at Burghley, in 2000. Despite countless wins at national one-day events and the smaller three-days, it took him until 2012 to pull off another four-star victory. But that one, again at Burghley, triggered a remarkable run that encompassed winning three-stars at Blenheim and Boekelo in Holland and the French four-star at Pau within two months. In 2013, he iced the cake, taking America's most prestigious horse trials, the four-star in Kentucky and then the German equivalent, Luhmühlen. A fourth Burghley win followed that autumn. The strength in depth of his horsepower was demonstrated by the fact that those five big wins came courtesy of four different horses.

A top rider needs good owners. Without them, none of it is viable without considerable personal wealth. At the core of Andrew's operation are Rosemary and Mark Barlow, Libby Sellar, Nicky and Robin Salmon and Paul Ridgeon.

Libby has owned horses that Andrew has ridden for more than 25 years and says that she has "loved every minute of it".

"I like to buy my horses at the start of their careers because Andrew is completely brilliant at bringing on young horses," she says. "He has an amazing talent for understanding the mind of a horse which is almost unmatched, and I think falling off rough little ponies in his childhood in New Zealand was an advantage to this end; he progressed that way by trial and error and had to work it out for himself.

"Andrew stands out as a rider because of his natural ability, but almost more importantly because of his hard work and application to detail. There is no short cut to fame and glory. Clearly he is a talented athlete, but it is his work ethic that stands him apart from many. He has a passion for his job that can make him seem somewhat hot-headed from time to time, but it is worth noting that if there is a dispute of any sort going on, then Andrew is usually proved to be right! I will always give him my vote."

Rosemary, a great supporter of both the British team and Andrew, whom she and her husband Mark have known since they sent him a fat, hairy Spinning Rhombus in 1987 to cure his habit of bucking everyone off and jumping out of every field he was put in, says: "His first thought is always of his horses, which is not the case with every rider. And he is very good with his owners. He always discusses the horses and any plans with us and we are made to feel involved. He is interested in our families and in our lives."

While Spinning Rhombus' infamous cricket score in the showjumping at the Barcelona Olympics was Rosemary's worst day in the sport, Avebury's Burghley victory in 2012 was the best.

Those triumphs at Burghley and Kentucky meant that he went to Badminton in 2013 bidding for the Rolex Grand Slam – a bonus of $350,000 paid to a rider who wins those events consecutively. It has only been won once, by Pippa Funnell in 2003. In a script that, if written by Jilly Cooper, would have been rejected by her publishers as too fanciful, there was, uniquely, another rider going for the Grand Slam at Badminton that year. It was William Fox-Pitt.

Between them, Andrew and William dominate eventing today, wrestling the world number one slot from each other. But they are not friends; Andrew is now married to William's first wife. There is great irony in how often the two riders have to share a podium and a press conference; how often they get almost identical marks in the dressage; how often they are drawn after each other in the running order.

Andrew and Wiggy have two children – Lily and Zach – to add to the two daughters, Melissa and Rebecca, he had with his first wife, Jayne.

Wiggy is best-placed to see the work that goes on behind the scenes, and to explain what makes him the person he is.

"Andrew has an enormous sense of belief in what he does and is capable of doing, and this is what he imparts to the horses he trains and to the riders he helps," she says. "He can make horse and rider believe they could fly if he tells them that's what is required.

She continues: "But he does not suffer fools gladly. Anyone who is lazy or incompetent, whatever their role, will find their relationship with him short-lived. He works extremely hard, to a high standard, and expects the same of others. His work ethic and stamina make him hard to keep up with, but engenders enormous respect from those that work with him.

"He doesn't spoon-feed the young riders who come to work for us, but expects them to open their eyes and learn every day, as much by watching as from riding, as he did himself. More young people have left Andrew and gone on to have successful careers of their own than from any other top event rider's yard, and that is a great legacy aside from his own competitive achievements.

"It is an uphill battle to get him to reduce his workload, and realise sometimes less can be more. He rarely takes a break, though I appreciate sometimes it's physically easier on the body to keep going. To that end he will ride every day, even out of season, when the yard is always full enough with horses.

"He once suggested going cross-country schooling on Christmas Day, saying the ground was perfect and there wouldn't be anyone else there..."

Andrew's career has featured frequent brushes with authority. "He hasn't always endeared himself to the people who run the sport," says Jenny Macarthur. "He was the McEnroe of eventing; he had trouble buttoning his lip and couldn't help speaking out when things weren't right."

Age and experience have taught him to control his temper. But thunder flashes still appear when he is riled. An example of this came in the spring of 2014, when an interview peppered with expletives made it on to the national television news in New Zealand.

There is, however, a softer side behind the battle-hardened exterior. Andrew has great charm and a very good – in the dry, understated way of his countrymen – sense of humour. He holds intently the gaze of anyone he is talking to, and his smile lights up a room. "I couldn't have wished for better friends than Andrew and Wiggy when my mother was ill," says Annabel Scrimgeour. "There's a very compassionate side to Andrew that people don't necessarily see."

Oliver Townend, who is some 20 years his junior, regards him as one of his closest friends. "I first met him at an event in France in 2001," says Oliver. "Growing up, there were only two people I was interested in watching – Andrew and Mark Todd. When I was walking back to the stables after working my horse, he came up behind me, stuck his hand out and said: 'I'm Andrew.' I was eighteen, and I thought, if a man as famous as he is in my job can introduce himself to a young person, then that's how I should I should try to behave. It stuck with me and made a huge difference as to how I look at people in the same situation."

Andrew has been both friend and mentor to Oliver. At the end of 2011, Andrew passed Oliver the ride on Armada, a mercurial horse with immense talent, and was delighted when the pair finished second at Badminton in 2014.

People in the sport have watched Andrew's development as a rider over the years. Ian Stark, a much-medalled British event rider and now trainer and course-designer, says: "He has always been very brave and competent, but he has got better and better with age and experience, and now is a top-class, very elegant rider. He is a serious contender to win at any level on any horse. I have huge respect for him – he's a very talented individual."

Andrew has no plans to scale down his competing any time soon. "Experience counts for so much," he says. "Young people can be very courageous and throw caution to the wind, which should be encouraged – they must have that will to win and bravery to do it – but the knowledge you have acquired when you are older and have done a lot gives you a big head start over younger riders."

The only part of his job Andrew now finds tiresome is the travelling. "But it has to be done," he says. "I certainly have the drive to continue riding. I am very lucky to have a career which I want to get up in the morning to do."

GROWING UP IN NEW ZEALAND

I WAS BORN IN 1961 AT KIHIKIHI, near Te Awamutu on in North Island, the third of six children. Picture 1 shows all six of us in 1971: (left to right) Jamie, then aged eight, Helen (eleven), John (thirteen), Sarah (one), Liz (four) and I'm on the far right, aged 10, looking rather suspicious of the whole thing. I think I was a fairly awkward child and very stubborn – and still am!

1.

2.

3.

Picture 2 is of my mother Heather and I at my first competition – winning the Beautiful Baby competition at Kihikihi. The bashed nose came later, after an encounter with a swing when I was three. My father left when I was young and I've had nothing to do with him since. My mother was an amazing woman who did a brilliant job of bringing the six of us up on her own. She was a teacher, and a popular and well-known figure in the local area who died in 1998 when taken ill on a visit to England to watch me ride.

I grew up on a 120-acre dairy farm, and from the age of about 10 my job was to feed the calves. Picture 3 of me and my pet calf, Cathy, was taken in 1968 on "Pet Day" at school, which was a big thing – most kids on farms had a calf or a lamb.

I wasn't keen on being at school. There was so much to do at home, and that interested me much more. After my father left, my mother took over running the farm. There was a massive mortgage on the property and we all worked the farm together, milking, making silage and hay – everything that comes with running a dairy farm.

When, after a couple of years, things were going well, the bank manager suggested to my mother that she did something for the children, like put in a swimming pool. She did – but we built it!

I didn't speak much, and I'd go to school and sit in silence. It just wasn't as exciting as being at home, catching eels and frogs in the drain. Whenever I played sport at school I was very competitive, however – whether I knew what I was doing or not.

When I was 13, I was milking our neighbour's cows before school because he had broken his leg, and although my teacher knew I was being genuine because he could see the cowshit on my arms, I was sent to the headmaster to explain why I had been late so many mornings in a row. He asked me how much money I was making doing it. I told him, he did the sums in his head and suggested I carried on!

Pictures 4 and 5 are of me on my pony, Rose Of Tralee. She wasn't a beauty but she was good fun, and after my first pony Rajah she was like a Rolls-Royce. Both my parents had ridden to school every day, but that was all the riding they did. We children all rode though, and first I got a coloured pony called Rajah who bucked me off all the time. The only thing I learnt from him was how to get back on: once he'd bucked me off he'd put his head down to eat, I'd sit on his head and tap his jaw, he'd put his head up and I'd wiggle back down his neck. He only bucked when I tried to canter, so for a while I thought that's how cantering worked!

My mother swapped Rajah for Rose with some local Maori boys. Rose didn't buck me off and she could jump, which was a considerable improvement. We lived next door to where the Pony Club rallies were held, so we used to sneak over and bomb around the jumps. We never rode on roads and loved galloping about playing cowboys, trying to "bulldog" yearling dairy calves, for which we got into huge trouble if we were caught.

It was so different to learning to ride in the UK nowadays – children were able to enjoy far more freedom. We joined the Pony Club, but we wouldn't have been any instructor's ideal pupils. If one of us got fed up and went home, we'd all just scarper as well.

When I was about 12, we started hunting, hacking about five miles to the meets. It was nothing like hunting in Britain – the Te Awamutu Hunt Club didn't have any hounds, just a master who was a racing fanatic whose children were in the Pony Club with us. He led, and everyone

5.

else tagged along behind, jumping fence after fence for about an hour and a half.

We were crossing dairy farms where each field was about three acres in size with a fence in and a fence out. Sometimes all we'd jump would be hedges; other times seven strands of wire with marking batons about every metre. I learnt at a young age to sit still on the approach to a fence and let the pony or horse pop over them.

When we started hunting we needed to get the ponies fitter, but we were too lazy to put the tack on, or even take the rugs off. We'd vault on, canter them round and round and then just get off and leave them panting away – not something you'd find in the Pony Club manual! At that age I definitely wasn't that into riding – the only class I could win at shows was the bareback jumping as I couldn't often be bothered to put a saddle on.

At one stage I wanted to be an auctioneer, because when I was little I'd go to lots of sales with my father and be in charge of selling a pen of sheep, or something. It was an odd ambition for a child who didn't say much, but I guess it was because the auctioneer was in charge of one of the things I enjoyed the most.

Picture 6 is of me on Heidi at the Waikato Pony Club Area Trials in 1976. She was originally my brother Jamie's pony and she was the first one I sold and made money on, which made me much more interested in the whole thing! Jamie didn't ride for long before taking up rugby instead, but he was very good at it – he excels at all sports. Helen rode quite a bit, and John, who is now a respected course-designer, was the keenest of all of us. He was interested in eventing and in doing it all properly. He is three years older than me, and I used to tag along with him to competitions and do the pony class.

I began to work out that I could quite easily make money from riding and selling horses. My mother encouraged us to do it – after all, it's a pretty good way of keeping teenage boys out of trouble.

Picture 7 was taken during my first year doing proper eventing when I was 15. I'm riding Cadet, an ex-racehorse that my brother John lent me for the Pony Club Trials. I managed to get on to the Waikato team, and after the championships I did some senior one-day events on him. I was useless at dressage and couldn't see any reason why you should do it – I was always being told that my horse was above the bit, which meant nothing at all to me at that stage.

When I was 15 I stopped going to school on Mondays and Fridays because in New Zealand you could get your driving licence at that age and I went off shoeing polo ponies to make money. I wasn't qualified to do so but my brother John had taught me how to shoe – he'd spent three months with a professional farrier when he was 16. I left school for good at the end of that year.

Picture 8 is Cadet and I at my first advanced event – the New Zealand national three-day event at Sherwood, near Hawkes Bay – when I must have been 17. I was put on the New Zealand squad for future championships with him and with another horse, Link, after this, as they'd both gone clear across country, but Cadet was sold

7.

and Link had a bad wire cut, so it didn't have much of an effect on me as I couldn't go any further with them.

That was the year that New Zealand sent an eventing team to the World Championships for the first time. The championships were held at Lexington in the USA, and five riders – Mark Todd, Joanne Bridgeman, Carol Harrison, Nicoli Fife and Mary Hamilton, went to represent New Zealand. Joanne Bridgeman, who had been in my Pony Club, did the best of the team riding a horse called Bandolier, which had belonged to one of my brother John's best mates.

The Waikato branch of the Pony Club put on a film of Lexington in the local village hall and for the first time I saw world-class eventing. I saw the likes of the American riders Bruce Davidson, Mike Plumb and Jimmy Wofford, wearing flash gear and riding nice horses, and I thought, "That looks like fun."

At this stage, I was working with John, producing ex-racehorses for sale to the competition market, and breaking in young National Hunt horses. In the mornings I rode out racehorses for local trainers. I didn't have many thoughts about the future – it was fairly obviously going to involve horses, as that was what I seemed to be good at, but I didn't spend much time thinking about it. However, one year on from this last photo, everything changed, and I started on the life course that has taken me to where I am today.

8.

FIRST IMPRESSIONS

MY FIRST BRITISH EVENT WAS AT CROOKHAM IN 1980, and funnily enough Bruce Davidson was riding there. He was the rider who had impressed me so much when I watched the film of the 1978 world championships back in the village hall at home. He won the individual title. For someone who had flown from the other side of the world with a five-year-old who hadn't done an event before, that was quite mind-blowing.

The thing that struck me most about eventing in Britain was how many people there were at the competitions. The sport in New Zealand at that time was very low-key, with only a handful of competitors and therefore very few hangers-on. On the cross-country course, there would be the starter and the jump judges, and that was it. Even if local events in Britain didn't attract the paying public, the much greater numbers of competitors brought with them a large crew of people and everything felt much busier.

WOODSTOCK

Arrival in England, 1980

THIS IS WOODSTOCK, who I brought with me to the UK when I first left home in 1980. The British racehorse trainer Derek Kent and Stanley Powell, who owned his yard near Chichester, had come over to New Zealand to buy horses to run over fences. They bought two five-year-olds from John. Stanley Powell saw Woodstock and in conversation I said I was planning on doing some events with him. He then said, "If you want to event, come to Britain and Derek will give you a job".

It was a pivotal day in my life and an incredible offer from Stanley; only later would I fully appreciate its significance.

A couple of weeks later, Woodstock and I were on a plane. I arrived on February 27, and hated it. It was cold, I didn't know anyone and didn't really have a clue what I was doing.

I barely knew where Britain was on the map. It took forever to get there. And on arrival I got lumbered with a big bill for VAT and import duty on the horse, which I had to pay before I could leave the airport. I'd used all my money to pay for my airfare so Derek Kent kindly lent me the money – and I was stuck in England already in debt.

It never occurred to me that Woodstock wouldn't be an event horse. That's what I wanted him to be, and so I presumed it would work like that! Actually, he was a lovely horse. I did five events on him – four novices and an intermediate – and sold him to Holland, where he went to the Young Rider European Championships. I kept him at the Powells' yard, riding him at lunchtime, and worked for Derek as a stable lad the rest of the time. Sue Gow, wife of Derek's assistant trainer, Robin, evented so she could explain to me how to enter events, and she drove me to them in a Land Rover and trailer.

As soon as I could sell Woodstock for decent money I did. I was desperate to get out of here and go home, but Stanley told me I'd be back in a month and he was right.

MARK TODD AND SOUTHERN COMFORT

Badminton, 1980

I KNEW MARK TODD because we lived quite near each other in New Zealand, and he and his horse Southern Comfort were on the same plane over as me and Woodstock, as was the Australian rider David Green, who later married Lucinda Prior-Palmer.

Mark was coming over to ride at Badminton for the first time and, during the flight, I asked if I could groom for him there. A few weeks later, there we both were. Neither of us had a clue what we were doing – but, much to the Brits' shock, he won. There was clearly nothing to this eventing thing!

I certainly couldn't plait or anything useful and I think I arranged for a girl who was grooming for someone else to plait the horse. Luckily Mark was pretty hands-on and did most of the grooming himself. It was a lot of fun, but I can't pretend I contributed much to his success.

SPIT-TEAK

Gatcombe, 1983

This is my first Gatcombe, the second year the event ran. It was the first time I won a prize (seventh place) in an advanced class. My dressage was rubbish, but we scorched round the cross-country and got a prize. I felt like I'd won it! You wouldn't find a fence like this now: if you wandered off your line you would land in a whole heap of trouble.

Spit-Teak was a New Zealand thoroughbred. He'd competed at novice level over there, and I'd brought him over to the UK the second year I was here, in 1981, with the idea of taking him to the Olympics. He had been going very well when he strained a tendon at Burghley in 1983; he had two years off, then came back to competition for a bit, but was never in the same league again.

TERIPAI

First Burghley, 1983

During my time at Stanley Powell's, they kindly invited me to live in the house and treated me as part of the family. I had Teripai to ride at that time, and scored my first British win on him, at South of England, in 1982. Teripai came to me because he'd been falling quite a bit. We got on pretty well together, but he did make some horrendous mistakes. These photographs were taken during the steeplechase at my first attempt at Burghley, in 1983. It looks as if I'm doing ballet! I landed on my head which hurt a lot and put me off going back to Burghley for a while.

Teripai belonged to the late Jenny Fountain, a mainstay of British eventing in the south of England, and the following season I moved up to her place near Guildford. Here, I met Jayne St John Honey, a member of the British Young Rider squad who lived a couple of miles up the road, whom I was to marry.

KAHLUA
AND RUBIN

First Badminton, 1984

New Zealand eventing had developed sufficiently by this stage for there to be a drive to get enough riders qualified to send a team to the Olympics for the first time. I needed a replacement horse after Spit-Teak went lame, which is where Kahlua (top picture below), stepped in. He was originally from New Zealand and I got him in December 1983. We had to go to Badminton to qualify and be selected for the team, which we did, despite him only being eight years old and not much of a showjumper.

Badminton was my first international event – something which wouldn't happen nowadays, as riders have to go through the grades (from one-star level) to qualify for a four-star event like this – but we went clear inside the time across country and I thought eventing was easy! It seems unbelievable now, but I only did four or five events on him in total – our next competition after Badminton was the Los Angeles Olympics.

Rubin (pictured below), my other Badminton ride that year, was so strong that I had to do a circle in the Lake and, at the Ski Jump, I had to use both hands on one rein to turn him, so we picked up a couple of stops.

Rubin belonged to Jenny Fountain, who had bought him from a businessman called Ashley Brodin. Ashley and I developed a good arrangement whereby I'd do two events on his horses and then he'd do two. My job was to tune them up so he would have an enjoyable day's competing. Ashley looked after me very well and bought nice horses.

Another early owner of mine was Nick Hebditch, a chicken farmer. I got the ride on a horse called Schiroubles – because no one else would ride it – and before long Nick had four horses with me. The first British three-day event I ever won was on a horse of his, Fast Polisher, at Osberton in 1990.

KAHLUA

Los Angeles Olympics, 1984

Kahlua was quite a chunky horse; he definitely wasn't full thoroughbred, more of an old-fashioned hunter type. However, he was very, very honest on the cross-country because I didn't really know what I was doing and nor did he. I look like a monkey up a pole here and that was an improvement on how I looked at Badminton.

I was only 23 and pretty over-awed by being at an Olympics – and also by the size of the cross-country, which was held some way out of Los Angeles at the Fairbanks Ranch Country Club. The course seemed a lot bigger than Badminton, perhaps because it was on mown grass like a golf course.

It was also hot and, as these were the days of long-format eventing (with a steeplechase phase and two roads and tracks phases before the cross-country), we were asking a lot. However, Kahlua did his best and was clear across country with some time-faults. He walked straight

through one quite tricky combination where we had to jump off a steep bank with three or four strides to a big fence where you had several options. I "bravely" took the option straight ahead of me and he hit it hard, but luckily I stayed on top. The picture opposite shows the water jump; it doesn't look much now, but I'd never seen a stretch of water that size before.

I like to say I helped my team-mate Mark Todd win his first individual gold medal – I jumped all the jumps where he told me to, and then he could see what worked and what didn't! I'm not sure I jumped them quite like he did though...

Kahlua jumped a better showjumping round in the vast Olympic arena than he had at Badminton and we finished halfway down the field. The next day I sold him to an American young rider and I think all three girls in the family competed him. He was a no-frills, plain, ordinary horse but one who got me going on the right path.

NEW ZEALAND

Winter, 1984

At the end of the 1984 eventing season, I went back to New Zealand for a couple of months. Jayne and I got married out there and returned to the UK around Christmastime. These pictures show me schooling a couple of the thoroughbreds my brother John bought off the racetrack to turn into competition horses.

MAKING
IT WORK

AFTER THE EXTRAORDINARY UNREALITY OF THE LOS ANGELES OLYMPICS,
it was time to get to work and turn eventing into a proper job. It was tough,
breaking into a sport that was largely the preserve of reasonably wealthy
people in a foreign country. There was no solution except a lot of very hard
work 18 hours a day in all weathers with few facilities. There was no question
of being selective about horses – I rode anything and everything I could.

MALIBU II

Badminton, 1985

THE YEAR AFTER LOS ANGELES, I tried to do the same thing again: buy a cheap horse, take it to Badminton and prepare it for the next Olympics. Only it didn't quite work like that.

Malibu, so called because I was working as a barman at the time and he was the same colour as the drink, hadn't done much and was, like Kahlua, only eight years old – nowadays, it's quite rare to see even a nine-year-old horse at a four-star. He jumped the first half of the course clear, but he mentally ran out of puff and had two falls.

The first came when he knuckled over on landing after a fence; then, two jumps later, I tried to turn him off the Vicarage Vee because we were on a horrendous stride and I realised we wouldn't get over it. As I turned, he jumped from a standstill and landed in the ditch. We finished, though; those were the good old days when you could just keep going after a fall. The sport has changed so much since then – even with two falls we ended up halfway up the order!

After Badminton, I took him to the three-day event at Waregem in Belgium, where he went well, but he picked up an injury after that and retired from eventing. Malibu had a lot of class: to do two long-format three-day events in a short space of time as an eight-year-old shows how genuine he was.

You couldn't do that in the modern sport, and I'm not sure whether that's a good or bad thing. I guess I was lucky to be eventing in that era and therefore able to do enough events to learn quickly. Malibu was big and brave with a good jump and nice movement, but I was very naïve in thinking I could fast-track any horse I wanted. I soon learnt that eventing wasn't quite as easy as I had thought.

CARIBOU

1986

Caribou was a brave little thing, only 15.3hh, and a lovely jumper who got to advanced level very quickly. He was a major income provider: I bought him cheaply and sold him well to Canada, where he ended up winning a team silver medal at the Pan-Am Games.

In 1985, Jayne and I moved to Buckingham and rented stables from the eventer Charlotte Steel. I made several contacts through her – lots of foreign buyers would drop in to see her – and she kindly directed some horses and owners my way, which is how I got Spinning Rhombus.

Mark and Rosemary Barlow, who were friends of the Steels, had bought him out of *Horse & Hound* as a hunter, but he was being very naughty with their girl groom and jumping out all over the place. He came to me for a couple of weeks to be sorted out, and I think it was four years before he went home for a break!

Jayne played a huge part in our burgeoning business, doing the entries, riding a few horses every day and quite a lot of the day-to-day running of the yard.

SOCRATES

Portman, 1987

SOCRATES WAS ANOTHER GOOD EARNER! He came, probably out of racing, via the dealer and breeder Donal Barnwell, now well known for collaborating with William and Pippa Funnell in their Billy Stud enterprise. I got him at the time of the football World Cup and called him after one of the Brazilian players. Jayne rode him to start with and, like lots of thoroughbreds, it took him a little time to learn what to do and to become brave enough, but once he got it, he was consistent and won plenty.

I sold him for a good profit to a Canadian rider who took him to the Pan-Am Games. I had nearly sold him to Mark Todd the year before, but his vetting wasn't quite clean enough and Mark thought it was a bit too much of a risk, so I kept him for another year and made a fair bit more money as a result.

SEATTLE

Tetbury, 1988

SEATTLE WAS SO NAMED because he was lucky to "See At All"... I was based at Roger Stack's yard in Surrey from 1986 to 1988, riding his breakers for him. Roger, who was a top showing man, bought Seattle at Malvern Sales as a three-year-old to be a show horse but he bucked an awful lot. I used to ride him three times a day and still he bucked and bucked.

Roger and I went halves on him because we thought that any horse who could buck like that felt like he had to be athletic. He was basically a kind, gentle horse but it felt as if someone had "played" with him and it had gone wrong before we got him. By the end of his four-year-old year, as long as you were sensible and slow with him, he'd stopped bucking, although the last time he did it, he slammed his head down so hard that he broke both reins.

One day I noticed he had a weepy eye, which turned out to be a painful disease that makes horses blind, periodic opthalmia. He went to an eye specialist, who saved the eye from being removed, but he lost the sight in it. As a result I never thought that anyone would buy him, but he turned out to be a very successful horse.

Tomi Gretener, a Swiss rider who lived in the UK and trained the Japanese eventing team before the Seoul Olympics, rang me and asked if I'd sell him to one of his Japanese riders. He went for a lot of money, which was pretty good for a one-eyed horse. However, I think I might have looked after him too much when I rode him, as I never turned him with his blind eye leading. He must have been quite reliant on me to be his "eye", and I think the Japanese rider found it difficult.

SCORPION

Badminton, 1989

AT THIS STAGE IN MY LIFE I still thought anything with two ears and a tail could go to Badminton! As you can see, the horse looks as shocked by it as I do. We pulled up two-thirds of the way round.

Scorpion was quite chunky, by the Irish Draught stallion King Of Diamonds, and probably not overly fit – in those days the steeplechase was 4½ minutes long. I jumped in at the deep end with him and shouldn't really have taken him there. This sort of picture would be a no-no these days, but back then that was the sport. People wanted to see thrills and spills and were less concerned by pretty pictures.

By this stage, Jayne and I had bought a place in Somerset, near Yeovil, which seemed a long way away from everywhere I knew. We started there with five horses and two owners; when we sold up 10 years later, we were up to 40 horses at certain stages. We didn't have enough stables for all of them, so sometimes we'd have them sleeping on the horse-walker and living in the lorry during the day. We had two smart stables, and every owner thought that their horse lived in the smart stables...

SPINNING RHOMBUS,

Kings Somborne, 1989

SPINNING RHOMBUS, NICKNAMED "PIGGY", arrived at my yard in 1987 as a six-year-old. He was only supposed to come for a couple of weeks to sort out his bucking, but I suggested to his owners, Rosemary and Mark Barlow, that he did some events to keep his mind occupied. Straightaway he loved it. I just thought of him as this tubby little horse, but now that I think back, he took everything I asked in his stride. His stand-out quality was that he never got tired – the further he went across country, the faster he got. He met challenges – and the pain barrier – head on, yet he had none of that to offer when you looked at him.

He did some novices that year, winning two of them, and was advanced by the end of his seven-year-old season. This picture was taken at his third advanced event.

He wasn't a naturally flash dressage horse – and I wasn't a naturally flash dressage rider – but he was very good in his mind in the arena. He took no notice of crowds or anything like that. However, his determination on the cross-country didn't work so well in the showjumping arena. He had the same attitude – he just wanted to get to the other side of the fence – and he didn't really care how he got there.

SPINNING RHOMBUS

Punchestown, 1990

THIS WAS MY FIRST THREE-DAY EVENT VICTORY, handily the year of the World Equestrian Games in Stockholm. Spinning Rhombus and I had produced a reasonable dressage test, and were due to go across country right at the end of the day. There had been falls and eliminations all day long and, after whizzing round the steeplechase, I could hear all the problems over the commentary while we were on the roads and tracks. I kept thinking that if I concentrated and rode properly, he could go clear and fast round this course, and I'd been told that to be in contention for selection for Stockholm I needed to do very well.

There was a difficult water fence early on with a wavy brush bounce into it that meant you didn't see the water until you'd taken off at the second brush. It had caused loads of stops and falls. But because Spinning Rhombus wasn't a very careful horse, he wasn't going to worry what was on the other side. He did it all very well and

was lightning-fast, so we finished cross-country day in the lead, which was the first time I had been in that position at a three-day event.

I did get quite nervous before the showjumping. He wasn't a great showjumper and this really mattered. But I had a few fences in hand, and in the end I only used up one of them. He was quite young then and I think he was a bit shocked by the height of the fences and therefore jumped very well.

In those days, Punchestown was the stepping stone to Burghley later in the year, and was a high-class competition that produced winners who went on to great things. The Irish have a way of making you feel like you've won the Olympics and it was all very exciting. I've always been a big fan of Punchestown's course-designer Tommy Brennan; he was a real horseman who rode in the 1968 Olympics and an incredibly creative thinker, talker and course-designer.

CAMEL RACING

Ston Easton, 1990

THE ORGANISERS ASSURED US WE DIDN'T NEED REINS! I think we're even galloping in the wrong direction to the finishing line. At the time, this camel felt a bit classier than some of horses I was riding...

STOCKHOLM WORLD EQUESTRIAN GAMES

1990

STOCKHOLM WAS MY FIRST APPEARANCE on a New Zealand team since Los Angeles. LA had gone way over my head but by Stockholm I knew what it was about, and therefore appreciated it more.

This time, the New Zealand team wasn't going for a "cup of tea and a look around" anymore. Mark Todd (right) and Blyth Tait (second left), who had come over from New Zealand the year before, were on top form and we were in with a chance of winning team gold. I didn't think I would be selected for the team, but I'd just won Punchestown on Spinning Rhombus and I'd been to the test event at Stockholm the year before and had gone well, so I was chosen along with Andrew Scott (left), a rider who was mainly based back in New Zealand.

I was the first of the team to go across country and knew I had to go well round what was the biggest track I'd ever attempted. The roads and tracks section took place on proper, tarmac roads, which took it out of the horses, and the cross-country was very long. Not many went clear, but Spinning Rhombus finished clear inside the time. I thought I was six seconds over – I'm sure I was told the wrong optimum time! Perhaps I should have bothered to check what it was myself...

Spinning Rhombus came out of it very well; he was always keen on his grub and he won the prize for the best conditioned horse. We would have won an individual medal, had he not had three showjumps down, but that was pretty good for him.

Blyth won the individual gold medal on Messiah. I ended up fourth individually – my least favourite finishing position, but pretty good nevertheless – and Mark was fifth on Bahlua, a horse he'd bought from me. We won team gold – our country's first – and started the "New Zealand domination" which was to last a decade.

APPLAUSE

Bramham, 1991

I sold Applause as a four-year-old for a quick profit but six months later he was back because he'd turned very nappy. I rode him in his first couple of events in 1988, then Jayne took over and won a few novices on him and I got back on once he was ready for intermediate. He was a consistent winner and because he had had bad X-rays of both hocks, which didn't seem to worry him, he was in no danger of being sold so became part of the furniture.

He didn't start life as a natural jumper, but he went for 18 months at advanced level without having a pole down. Then the Dutch rider Eddy Stibbe asked if I'd sell him. I told him about the X-rays, but he bought him for his wife Mandy anyway and he was the reserve horse for the Dutch team for the Barcelona Olympics. Applause had been winning me money, so I didn't sell him cheap!

Shortly after this picture was taken we were actually eliminated after falling in the water, but he was sixth at Burghley that autumn, going clear inside the time across country. Applause was the first horse I won an advanced class on at Weston Park, in 1990. Weston became a very happy hunting ground for me: in both 2006 and 2010 I won three advanced sections in one day, and I must have won 15 or 16 or so in total there.

PARK GROVE

Blenheim, 1991

PARK GROVE IS THE HORSE who got me connected with Ramon Beca, who at the time was a member of the Spanish team. He went on to breed many of the horses I compete now and has become a great friend and supporter.

Park Grove was a Dutch-bred horse Eddy Stibbe sold to Ramon, who needed a replacement for his Olympic horse, Count De Bolebec. Park Grove had been produced by Caroline Pratt when she was based at Roger Wright's yard – his horses were prefixed "Park" – and she'd won quite a bit on him. He could really move and jump, but he could also stop – very suddenly.

He and Ramon didn't really gel, and as I lived near to where Ramon kept him at Sorrell Warwick's yard, he asked me to compete him. At first, Park Grove would stop in the showjumping with me, and you knew that if you did anything wrong he'd punish you very harshly for it. You had to keep hold of his head or he'd stop, but he was very classy.

I won the inaugural Blenheim Horse Trials on him, in 1991, and, after only doing a couple of events in 1992, I won three advanced classes on the trot with him in 1993. His legs had had a lot of mileage and didn't stand up to work for very long but it was the start of a long and happy association with Ramon.

JUMBO

Le Lion d'Angers, 1991

THIS IS CAROLYN BATES' STALLION JUMBO, who went on to be a legendary sire of event horses, including my dual Burghley winner Avebury.

I'd started riding him in March that year. He looked big and heavy compared with most eventers – he was three-quarters Irish Draught – but to sit on he was a very agile, nice-moving horse with a fabulous gallop stride for his build and very light on his feet. He wasn't fast, but could go from A to B at a reasonable speed. He finished sixth overall at Le Lion d'Angers in the two-star and was the highest-placed young horse.

The following year we went to Boekelo three-star in The Netherlands. He only got one time-fault on the steeplechase and perhaps two on the cross-country, and this is where horses like Avebury get their speed from. A lot of Jumbo's progeny are like him in that their gallop can be deceiving. His main asset was that he could jump out of the rhythm you had in a very controlled manner, so you didn't waste time setting up for fences.

After Boekelo we stopped eventing him, as he was being sent 60 to 70 mares a year and he seemed too valuable to event. He went showjumping with William Funnell and I think he got to Grade A before going to the dressage rider Jennie Loriston-Clarke and reaching prix st georges level, so it's no fluke he's been such a successful eventing stallion.

Jumbo helped me in my career because when I started riding him, I'd never had a horse who moved like him on the flat, and he made me realise what a good-moving horse felt like. He also taught me a lot about dealing with stallions, as he was the first one I competed. I soon realised I couldn't work him like the geldings. Once he knew what it was all about, he wouldn't gallop uphill, so I had to go flat out downhill and trot him back up!

All the "Jumbos" I've had since have been very similar to him. He was a notably good ditch jumper and the first time I've taken any of his offspring cross-country schooling, they've jumped ditches beautifully.

SPINNING RHOMBUS,

Barcelona Olympics, 1992

I WAS NUMBER THREE out on the cross-country course and the first of the New Zealand team to go. The course was long and very big – it was one of the last enormous Olympic tracks – and I really wanted to go the direct routes everywhere.

Lots of riders were concerned about this jump into water. I wasn't – I was more worried about the big verticals as Spinning Rhombus wasn't terribly careful. Not many riders took the straight route here – possibly because they watched us and thought it looked too hairy!

Basically, Spinning Rhombus tried to knock it down – it felt like he didn't get off the ground. It was a proper, solid stone wall and I lost both stirrups, dropped the reins and thought for a minute that I was going swimming. But his neck stayed out in front of me and when he landed, I sat back as though nothing had happened and off we went.

He sped around in the second-fastest time. The conditions were really hot and, as we'd been lectured about the heat and not going mad on the cross-country, I left

it a bit late to start winding up the pace. Actually there was a constant breeze, being up in the mountains, and he wasn't tired at all; now I know more, I would ride differently and have gone faster at the start of the course. The next day he jumped the showjumps like he did that stone wall – but they came down.

Spinning Rhombus always found the showjumping difficult, but before Barcelona he'd jumped clear at several advanced events in a row.

I knew in the warm-up I had a serious problem. After the second jump Spinning Rhombus hit every single fence like he'd never done before. We went into the arena, with eight fences in hand to give New Zealand the gold medal over Australia. We had nine down. I was angry, humiliated and conscious that I had let my team and country down. It wasn't the individual medal that mattered – I'd discounted that – it was the team's. It was the worst day of my career.

We'd won the team silver medal, but it felt as if we'd won nothing.

ONWARDS
AND UPWARDS

ALTHOUGH THE BARCELONA OLYMPICS HAD BEEN A DISASTER, every cloud has a silver lining. Bringing Spinning Rhombus back out to Badminton and Burghley the following year and achieving top results with him was a major turning point in my career. It taught me to think laterally to get the best out of horses, and people recognised what I achieved with Spinning Rhombus against the odds. It led to me being offered a higher class of horse to ride than I had been previously: horses that had their problems, but with whom, once I had worked out what made them tick, I could be very competitive at the top events.

JAGERMEISTER II

Gatcombe, 1993

THIS WAS THE FIRST YEAR that Gatcombe hosted the British Intermediate Championships, and when I entered Jagermeister – who was quite young, at seven, to be there – I didn't think much of it. Afterwards, I soon realised it was quite something to win a class at Gatcombe; it's British eventing's summer highlight, and the national championships, and owners love going there. In the picture I'm flanked by Robert Lemieux and Tina Gifford (now Cook), who were second and third, with Howard Robinson of the sponsor Calor Gas.

Since then I've found out how hard it is to win any of the championship classes at Gatcombe, although I've had a lot of luck in the normal advanced sections. Generally my novices, who start their careers at novice level aged five, are too young to win, although I've had lots of placings. Avebury was second in the novice championships in 2007 and both he and Nereo were fourth in the intermediate championships.

I tend to use the British Open to prepare for other events, often just doing the dressage and showjumping phases, although in 2011 Nereo and Avebury finished first and second in it. That was a good weekend – Quimbo and Calico Joe won the two advanced classes as well.

SPINNING RHOMBUS

Burghley, 1993

ONE GOOD THING CAME OUT OF THAT disastrous day at the Olympics in Barcelona; it led to me meeting Spanish rider Luis Àlvarez de Cervera, who would later on as a trainer play a great part in my success.

He was the only person who offered me any help afterwards. He had competed in Barcelona in both the showjumping and the eventing, which requires exceptional skill and has rarely been seen. He had his event horses at Waterstock, a centre run by the leading Swedish trainer Lars Sederholm, and a few weeks later he came up to me and said he'd fully understand if I wasn't interested, but he felt he could help – and would like to.

I took Spinning Rhombus up to him and he jumped on and had a ride. That's when I learnt that the horse could jump ten jumps really well, but that that was his limit. He was great with Luis for the first ten fences and Luis was smiling, but his smile slowly disappeared as Spinning Rhombus started knocking them down. As he hopped off, he said that if he hadn't seen the horse go across country with his own eyes, then he'd never have believed it was possible.

Luis suggested ways to ride the horse and things to do, and would ring with ideas as they occurred to him. I tried them, and took Spinning Rhombus to Boekelo, where he had five fences down. After that, I never jumped a single showjump on him unless it was in the ring.

The next year we had the second fence down at Badminton, which was my fault. I'd got nervy about not having done a single practice jump and suddenly the fences looked very big, but he was clear around the rest of the course.

Having gone across country the day before, we are all taught how important it is to make the horse supple and shorten up their stride again before the showjumping, so it's very difficult to go into the ring without having a warm-up. The first fence looks enormous when you canter over the start line! You can only do this with a very experienced horse, of course, but I try it every now and then these days – it sharpens you up and I'd recommend it to other riders.

At Burghley that autumn Spinning Rhombus was third after cross-country, and I said to Mark Todd, who was in second place behind the American rider Stephen Bradley: "You're going to feel more pressure than you've ever felt before!" "Why's that?" he asked. "Because I'm going to jump clear," I replied. He laughed – and I was joking. But we did jump clear. Unfortunately, so did Mark and Stephen! But third place – and we were the only pair to finish on our dressage score – was nearly as good as winning. Barcelona had been awful for Rosemary and Mark Barlow, but this was vindication for their horse.

The change in the horse's body language was unbelievable. I wouldn't have thought it was possible for a horse to alter so much – he went from feeling as if he was going to eat every fence, charging at them, to being elegant and light and assessing everything he was going to jump. It was extraordinary.

JAGERMEISTER II

Hexham, 1994

because it was through him that I met Libby Sellar, who went on to become an owner and a major support to me. Libby's daughter Amy was over here from New Zealand to event and bought a novice horse from me. After two years, she was going to university, so the horse came back to me to be sold again. Jagermeister was one of Amy's horses from New Zealand and the idea was that he came to the UK for her to ride while she was at university.

He arrived while I was away at the Barcelona Olympics in 1992, and within a few days Amy had a terrible car crash from which it took her a long time to recover. By the time she was better, Jagermeister had reached advanced level and had turned from being a gentle, "girly" horse to one who pulled like a train and was very opinionated!

He was a very small horse whose mother was half-pony, while his sire was a German showjumping warmblood. He was a really good jumper and a nice mover, but he wanted to go everywhere as fast as he possibly could and hated being on his own. He competed at a World Equestrian Games and an Olympics, but it got to the stage where the jumps weren't big enough to slow him down.

When he retired, he went back to New Zealand and my niece Jodie showjumped him. Despite the fact that Jodie had just come off ponies, they were very successful and jumped in two World Cup qualifiers. I couldn't believe he could jump that big! There can't be many horses that have been to a world championships and an Olympics in eventing and gone on to jump in World Cup classes. He was probably twenty by then but his attitude hadn't changed: he loved working.

After that, he went to Libby's farm manager's children and got their showjumping careers up and running. It was only in 2013 that he finally retired altogether, in his mid-twenties, and he remains at Libby's farm, acting as a nanny to her young ponies.

MEMENTO

Moreton Morrell, 1994

MEMENTO WAS A MARE I BOUGHT with five others at Malvern Sales. She'd been a useless racehorse, called Bairn Free, but she was a nice mover and jumper. I paid £900 for her. She only did four events – we discovered that she had a very bad cataract in one eye – and this is her first, which she won on a dressage mark of 19. It wouldn't have been easy to sell her, so I thought I'd breed from her. She's the only broodmare I've ever had – and I only did it to bring my rates down. If I could say that part of my business was breeding horses, I had to pay the government considerably less!

The stallion Jumbo was with me to compete at the time, so I covered her with him. She had three foals, all by Jumbo – Freckles, who I sold to Germany and who won a CCI**, a very small filly who I gave away, and Avebury (pictured below left as a foal).

I then gave Memento to Mark Chamberlayne, who bred Tristar II, on whom I won at advanced level, another advanced horse called Tomaz Gudanov whom Dan Jocelyn rides, and a filly who is producing foals by Jumbo herself.

In that bunch of horses from Malvern Sales was also Splendid Style. I bought him in October, started eventing him in March and by the end of that year he'd won nearly 100 British Eventing points. I sold him to the Dutch rider Eddy Stibbe.

JAGERMEISTER II

World Equestrian Games
at The Hague, 1994

NEW ZEALAND WAS HOT FAVOURITE to win the team competition in The Hague, so perhaps it was inevitable that it was all going to go horribly wrong. This was an incredibly hot and humid World Equestrian Games and the cross-country was held out of town, on heathland which had dry, dead sand. I was first to go for the team and was spinning round the cross-country quite happily on Jagermeister until we got to the water complex.

It was quite a difficult jump in, then you went a long way through the water before either jumping up a high bank and bouncing out over some vertical rails, or going a bit further to a smaller bank with one stride to some rails.

Jagermeister was always pretty strong once he'd seen a fence and, although he had no problem jumping into the water, he spotted the bank a long way off and took off way, way too far away from it. As a result, he didn't quite make it on to the bank, rammed himself headfirst into the rails and it all fell apart. In those days you could carry on after a fall, so I got back on and jumped round the rest of the course perfectly alright.

Mark Todd was last to go for the team on a good horse called Just An Ace. He took the other route in the water and then did exactly the same thing as me. Blyth Tait had already had an early fall with Delta, who got tired in the deep sand, and retired as well.

However, Vaughn Jefferis saved New Zealand honour and won individual gold for us on Bounce. The only good thing we could say about the whole competition was that we showjumped well and managed to get qualified as a nation for the next Olympics.

BUCKLEY PROVINCE

Burghley, 1995

BUCKLEY PROVINCE ARRIVED THE DAY after Cartoon II and, between them, they taught me a lot. I'd been asked to ride him at Badminton in 1994 when his jockey Lynne Bevan broke her collarbone and I agreed, but the powers that be at Badminton wouldn't let me – they said it had to be a British rider because the foreign rider allocation was full. So Graham Law rode him at Badminton, but the owners sent him to me after that.

Buckley Province wasn't a brave horse and it always felt as if he he didn't really want to be doing it. He was a very small thoroughbred – I could have virtually picked him up and carried him around. Lynne had done a lovely job on him, but he was a bit stiff through the shoulders and tended to jump with quite straight forelegs.

Lynne had always gone quite slowly on him, and part of that was probably because he wasn't the snappiest with his front legs at speed. I did the advanced at Gatcombe quite soon after getting him, and we fell twice! However, we got used to each other and went to Achselschwang, a German three-star in Bavaria, that autumn and won it.

We finished second at Saumur in the spring of 1995, but that July I managed to flip him over a big vertical rail into the water at Luhmühlen. It didn't seem to upset him unduly though, as we went to Burghley in September and he was foot-perfect all the way to give me my first four-star win. He felt much braver at the big events where he had to do the steeplechase before the cross-country; being thoroughbred, it didn't tire him, it just got his courage up and gave him some fluency in his jumping.

TWO TIMER

Open European
Championships at
Pratoni del Vivaro, 1995

ON TWO OCCASIONS – 1995 AND 1997 – the European Championships were held as Open competitions, which meant that teams from the USA, Australia and New Zealand could compete as well. In 1995 at Pratoni del Vivaro in Italy I think we perhaps didn't take it as seriously as we might have – or maybe we were just short of experienced horses, but apart from Vicky Latta on Chief, we were all riding relatively novice horses.

I ended up on a horse of Eddy and Mandy Stibbe's called Two Timer, who had originally been quite a good racehorse in New Zealand but hadn't done a great deal of eventing. I remember him giving me an unbelievable feel on the steeplechase: he could stand off a mile and land way beyond the fence, and I think we finished on our dressage score.

The New Zealand team were second behind the Brits – as we were again at Burghley two years later – and the medal ceremony became very confusing with European and Open European medals. When Mark Todd won the individual title in 1997, I think they thought better of including us in the European championship and dropped the "Open" bit from then on!

BUCKLEY PROVINCE

Atlanta Olympics, 1996

AFTER GOING WELL AT BADMINTON in the spring of 1996, Buckley Province and Jagermeister II were heading for the Atlanta Olympics where, at that stage in the sport, there were two competitions, team and individual, because the Olympic rules stated that you couldn't win two medals for one performance.

Jagermeister was picked for the team, with Blyth Tait (Chesterfield), Vicky Latta (Broadcast News) and Vaughn Jefferis (Bounce) and we ended up winning bronze. However, I felt I had a live chance of winning the individual competition on Buckley Province.

Atlanta, held in the sticky summer temperatures of the Deep South, was indeed very hot but not as bad as we had been warned it would be and the cross-country, designed by Roger Haller, was huge and long. However, as Buckley Province was little, fast and easy to turn, I thought it would suit him fine. The only thing he wasn't a big fan of was water jumps, but I didn't think this one would be a problem.

I was early to go on cross-country day, which should have been to my advantage, but just before I went word got back that blue dye had been put in the water jumps and that the first few riders had stopped at the first water complex, which was in the woods.

We got there, going well, and I put a bit more pressure on Buckley Province than I normally would, thinking the colour of the water would back him off. He jumped very high, perhaps startled by the bright colour, and just didn't put his front legs down in time. We fell and that was my Olympics done. I remounted and carried on – this picture is of the second water complex, which I jumped and then pulled up. All that was left was to congratulate Blyth on winning the individual gold with Ready Teddy and Sally Clark, another New Zealander, the silver on Squirrel Hill.

JAGERMEISTER II, BUCKLEY PROVINCE AND CARTOON II

1996

THIS PICTURE WAS TAKEN for a *Horse & Hound* feature and marks the first time I really had a team of horses capable of winning at the top. Between them they gave me confidence that I could be consistently successful; Jagermeister gave me my first Gatcombe title and Buckley Province my first four-star, and he and Cartoon II were the horses that first gave me an understanding of dressage. They had both been very well schooled by other people – Pippa Funnell and Lynne Bevan – and I was able to learn from them what dressage should and could feel like.

MR GLITZ

1996

I BOUGHT MR GLITZ AS A THREE-YEAR-OLD from Jayne's aunt, who had bred him. He was by Jumbo out of a mare by the National Hunt sire Town And Country and, until Avebury, he was the nicest Jumbo horse I'd ridden.

I could afford him because he bucked like anything when they started breaking him in! I sold him to Eddy Stibbe, who took over the ride when I'd got him to intermediate level and renamed him Earl Grey. After that, he became very strong with Eddy and I think was sold to America as a showjumper. He was a big, rangy horse who could move and jump, and if I had him now, I'd keep him and take him to the top. But in those days it was all about making a living.

CARTOON II

Burghley, 1996

CARTOON II WAS ONE OF MY FAVOURITE HORSES. He came from Pippa Funnell, and was typical of the very elegant horses she rode, but she'd had a few falls from him and thought it was time to let someone else have a go.

I won the first three events I did with him, but each time at some point on the cross-country I would land on his neck because he really wasn't clever with his legs.

After about four or five runs, the penny seemed to drop and he stopped clouting fences. He learned belief in going across country from me, but I learnt how to do dressage from him and he taught me an awful lot. Pippa had done a fantastic job in schooling him and he wanted to show off what he'd learnt – he was one hundred per cent focused on what you wanted him to do.

I'd never ridden a horse who could go on the flat like that and for a while I was nervous that I'd wreck him. I felt elegant in a dressage arena for the first time – not something I was used to! It was from Cartoon that I learnt that homework on the flat paid off, that if you did things properly, the dressage arena becomes a comfortable place for horses to be and they can relax in there. I now try to teach young horses at their first event that the arena is a safe place. I don't expect them to prance around being flashy; I want them to relax and enjoy themselves. If you don't put a young horse under any pressure, they will learn very quickly.

CARTOON II

Burghley, 1996

THIS PHOTOGRAPH LOOKS AS IF I'm casually taking a time-check, but in actual fact was a complete set-up. The *Horse & Hound* photographer Trevor Meeks had seen me doing it for real somewhere and, at Burghley, asked me when I was going to look at my watch. I said I'd do it whenever he wanted me to, to which he replied: "Just in front of Burghley House, please!" I was quite impressed that he trusted me enough to do it. It has become rather a famous picture.

Cartoon was second at Burghley that year, having been fourth the year before. I never really worried about him making mistakes in the jumping, even at four-star level, and he grew in confidence from that. He would go at whatever speed you asked and do anything you asked. Considering that he didn't have a lot of scope, he made it feel easy. Showjumping was his weak link – he jumped by Braille – and, like Spinning Rhombus, I never jumped him at home.

NEW YORK

Bramham, 1997

LIBBY SELLAR SAID she would buy me a horse, but she wanted it to be one from New Zealand. I was over at Puhinui horse trials and I saw New York working on the flat before competing in the novice class. I asked his owner, Gee Davison, if she'd sell him, and she agreed. He didn't have a great showjumping technique, but he was a nice, full-thoroughbred horse.

He was fourth at Blair Castle two-star in 1996 as a seven-year-old, and this picture was taken the following year at Bramham three-star. We were selected for the World Equestrian Games in Pratoni del Vivaro in 1998 and finished fifth individually,

but unfortunately we missed out on the being one of the team gold medal-winners because he had "tied up" the day after arriving in Italy and it was deemed too risky to put him in the team.

New York was a particularly good cross-country horse. He was fifth at Badminton in 1999 in horrendous wet weather and led after the cross-country at Burghley later that year but, sadly, went lame before the final horse inspection and had to be withdrawn. He wasn't in the same class as the horses I have now, but then he was certainly my top horse.

CARTOON II

Badminton, 1998

THIS IS A LOVELY PICTURE: Cartoon II looks so genuine and confident. The way he adapted himself on a big course was amazing. He taught me that if event horses have the right attitude and stay sound, they can learn to be very good. Calico Joe, one of my current horses, is an example of this.

This was a proper Badminton fence. Imposing, upright jumps like this stone corner make people ride well; if they don't, they come to grief. When riders have to think, they tend to ride more correctly. If the course-designer removes the necessity for the rider to think, it leads to sloppy riding and, as a result, either accidents or the wrong people winning because they've got a superb dressage mark and the cross-country doesn't play sufficient influence.

Horses will help you by backing themselves off when the profile of the fences encourages them to do so; when it's too invitingly easy, they pull harder. I miss the likes of Tom Smith's Walls and the Centre Walk Hedges at Badminton. They were tough, big fences, but very natural things for horses to jump. Now we have much more artificial obstacles and horses don't jump them so well or so naturally. The intensity of modern courses means they can catch out the good horses and good riders when they shouldn't.

MELISSA AND REBECCA NICHOLSON

1998

JAYNE AND I HAD OUR FIRST DAUGHTER, Melissa, on 30 June 1987, and Rebecca followed on 21 December 1990. They both rode a bit as children, as you can see from these pictures, but they didn't have great ponies, which meant they didn't find it particularly fun. They came to all the events with us – I like this picture of them cleaning my boots at Longleat in 1998 – and probably got fairly fed up with anything horsey. When Melissa was a baby and Jayne and I were both competing, there were occasions where she would get handed to the starter while we were on course! Rebecca took up riding again at home about ten years ago for a while when she had a boyfriend who played polo, and, to be fair to her, she can look pretty good! But I don't think the relationship lasted long and neither did her second riding phase.

In 1998 we sold our farm in Somerset and rented Patrick and Lucinda Darling's yard at Caradoc Court, near Ross-on-Wye, for a year, before moving to Woodlands Farm near Devizes in Wiltshire.

DAWDLE

Punchestown, 1998

DAWDLE WAS A LOVELY HORSE. He was owned by Jane Davies, whose son Mark died as a result of a fall at Burghley in 1988. Jane, along with her husband Michael, subsequently set up the Mark Davies Injured Riders Fund.

I'd ridden Dawdle's full-brother, Gumley, to advanced level. Gumley was beautiful, and a great mover and jumper, but he had fragile legs and broke down quite young. Dawdle was two years younger and nowhere near as big, but he was elegant. Unfortunately, he had fragile legs as well.

Here he is finishing second at Punchestown in 1998, having been third at Saumur and second at Blenheim – both three-stars – before that, and he was in the New Zealand team that won a silver medal at the Open European Championships at Burghley in 1997.

He was actually selected for the Sydney Olympics in 2000, and I took both him and New York out there. But New York went lame about a week after arriving in Australia, which meant that Dawdle – who was originally supposed to compete in the individual competition – was moved into the team. He passed the first vet inspection, but was lame the following morning!

Both Gumley and Dawdle were nappy horses, but once in the arena or start box they were very good. If I had both of them now, I could do a lot better with them. They were top-class, and, looking back, I probably used them up too much at low-key events rather than thinking of the bigger picture in the way I've learnt to do now.

Their full-sister, Waddle, was the dam of another of my top horses, Silbury Hill. This was probably the start of my interest in "families" of horses and the traits they share; I now tend to buy and ride a lot of horses who are closely related to each other. It gives me more insight into their characters and how to get the best from them.

MERILLION

Punchestown, 1998

MERILLION WAS OWNED by David and Jane Tolley who had a yard near Wantage in Berkshire. Matt Ryan had competed the horse to three-star level and I was sent him because he had become very strong on the cross-country.

Merillion was a superb mover, but quite tricky to jump. You had to be very tactful coming into a fence on him as he could easily flick his head up at just the wrong moment and this caused us to incur stupid run-outs at both Badminton and Burghley. Basically, however, he wanted to do the job well and I enjoyed riding him. This picture shows him coming fourth at Punchestown , two places behind Dawdle.

THE NIGHT BEFORE
THE COUNTRYSIDE MARCH

London, 1998

ROSEMARY BARLOW ORGANISED a fund-raiser before the Countryside March, a protest against the hunting ban, in London in 1998. Somehow, I was persuaded to join (from left) Blyth Tait, Ian Stark and the jockeys Chris Maude and Mick Fitzgerald in dressing up as the Village People. Our costumes were assembled by Badminton's press officer Julian Seaman – it certainly wasn't the sort of thing I had in my wardrobe!

Allan Curtis, who is a familiar face to many from the horse show at Olympia, taught us the dance, and I fear he took it rather more seriously than we did. I hadn't seen Mick and Chris for a while, but I'd known them quite well when they lived near me in Somerset. In fact, Mick nearly went and worked for my brother John in New Zealand – but near the time he was supposed to go he got a call from the trainer Nicky Henderson asking him to ride a few of his horses, and the rest is history.

WHITMONDAY

Windsor, 1997

THE ROADS AND TRACKS PHASES AT WINDSOR were always very pretty and coincided with the rhododendrons being out. Here I am going for a hack round Ma'am's garden! Whitmonday was a gigantic horse, about 18hh, who his owner and breeder Mark Chamberlayne had won a point-to-point on. He had also won a Burghley Young Event Horse qualifier with the showjumper Philip Tuckwell before that, so he was more educated than your typical point-to-pointer.

When Mark started winding down his riding career he sent Whitmonday to William Fox-Pitt, who didn't like him, and then to me. I must say that I didn't like him much either when I started jumping him! I'd never seen a thoroughbred so big, and I kept feeling he needed bigger fences to be able to balance himself properly. So I bravely stuck them up, and he jumped them very well and carefully. He was lovely to ride on the steeplechase phase and at three-day events when there was plenty of room between the cross-country fences because he could really use his

stride, and I remember the thrilling feeling of going round the steeplechase track at Punchestown where they used the real racecourse fences.

He was third at Punchestown in 1999, having gone really well at advanced level for two or three years. But two fences from home he went out like a light, and I was very relieved when we got to the landing side of the last jump. I took him straight to the vets, knowing something was wrong, and they found his heart was fibrillating. It had corrected itself by that evening and he showjumped clear the next day, but it happened again at Badminton in 2000 when he suddenly lost his gallop towards the end of the course.

The vets said that his heart was fine, but I wasn't convinced and the next day it felt as if he was struggling to jump the parallels and kept putting in extra strides everywhere. He was taken to Newmarket, where they put a heart monitor on him for 24hr, and it showed the heart had an abnormal rhythm several times in that period, so he was retired from eventing.

HEYERDAHL

Puhinui, 1999

HEYERDAHL WAS A CATCH RIDE that gave me a nice little bonus win. Puhinui is one of the major events on the calendar in New Zealand and in its early days the organisers would fly over international riders to compete on borrowed horses in the two-star section to give it a bit of publicity.

Puhinui is an unusual venue, right next to Auckland airport and the sea, and it used to get a really big crowd. It still runs a three-star section but doesn't get so many entries without the international riders and isn't such a spectacle.

It's still difficult for the riders who don't leave New Zealand to get experience of more competitive eventing. The best ones over there are those who have seen what riders in Britain, America and Australia are doing and who have maintained those standards once they have got back home and got some perspective on eventing in other countries.

MR SMIFFY

Burghley, 2000

AT THE END OF 1999, Paul Davies rang to ask if I'd be interesting in riding Mr Smiffy, a horse he owned with Janet Oliver. I knew the horse because Lucy Wiegersma had had him as a five-year-old when she spent a winter with me, and I'd seen him at events with first Rodney Powell and then J-P Sheffield, getting ever stronger and more wayward. I have to admit that one of the attractions of taking on the ride was that Paul's late partner Kenneth Clawson was the British team's showjumping trainer, and it was around the time that the British were complaining about the number of foreign riders in the UK. There were suggestions that we should pay more in registration fees and entries, which seems a bit rich considering that we contribute quite a lot to the eventing economy and event organisers are quite happy to use our names in publicity material. So to be asked to ride a British-owned advanced horse which had previously been ridden by a Brit amused me and seemed to fly in the face of the attitude towards us foreigners. I'd have had to have really disliked the horse not to accept the ride!

I agreed to ride Mr Smiffy at competitions and that Paul and Kenneth would keep him at home in between. I first rode him at Aldon, and I suggested to the owners that they didn't watch the first few runs, because they were going to be a learning experience for both of us. I wanted to work on the theory that if I let him run into trouble early on in the cross-country, he might realise that he had four legs and he ought to look after them. When he sped up, I kicked, which surprised him. When I could I left him alone and encouraged him to look after himself.

Our first three-day event together was at Saumur, which isn't ideal for strong horses as the course twists through the woods. The first half of the course was fine, but in the second half he got quite strong and strung out. But he felt perfectly safe – except at the finish, which was in the main arena and had concrete rails around it. When I asked him to slow down, he got faster and faster, latching onto the rails. I swung him off those only to find some tape in front of us, which he jumped, landing right beside the ground jury and the vet. He stopped dead and I quietly walked off as though that was exactly what I had planned to do.

Mr Smiffy was not naturally supple and always felt stiff through his body, but I felt we were heading in the right direction and so I took him to Burghley that autumn.

We won, but we're better remembered for the incident that gave rise to the "Mr Stickability" nickname than for the actual victory. It happened at the Waterloo Rails – vertical rails on undulating ground – and was as much my fault as his. Normally he'd tow you into a fence and you'd sit quietly. But he didn't this time and we found ourselves far too far off the fence, whereupon he put in an extra stride that there wasn't really room for. He did well to stay on his feet but went up vertically with his head between his feet. I was catapulted out of the saddle with my arms around his throat and my feet pointing towards the sky, but somehow ended up back in the plate.

It's quite a famous clip on Youtube now, and you can see a still from the video footage below, but at the time all that I thought was "Damn, I've dropped my stick and we've got a long way to go!" It woke both of us up and he was beautiful to ride after that. The pull-up at the finish is short at Burghley and that concerned me, but luckily he thought the deer fence was a bit big to jump.

SHEFF'S CHOICE WAS OWNED by Julian Trevor-Roper, who has always been a good friend of mine. In 1998, I was taking one horse to Pau for the two-star competition and he suggested I took Sheff's Choice as well. I'd never sat on him before and he arrived just in time to get on the lorry and go. Julian didn't come, he just handed me the tack and told me the horse was very easy.

He was right: he was beautiful to ride and we coasted through everything until I needed to pull up at the end of the steeplechase when I realised I hadn't had any say in anything up to that point and was just a passenger!

The cross-country was the same: he spun round very easily with his ears pricked but didn't listen to a thing I tried to tell him. I rang Julian and told him the bit Sheff's Choice had in his mouth wasn't really worth having and asked if the horse

showjumped in the same one. Julian replied that he did, which made me slightly nervous. But the horse did the same thing again, jumped clear and won. That's when he went from being called Sheff's Choice to Dish of the Day...

I told Julian to sell the horse while he was worth decent money, but he was far too attached to "Monty" so I rode him from time to time in the next couple of years, and we won Boekelo together in 2001. He eventually found his way to Italy, like quite a lot of my horses, and I'm fairly sure he's still there, aged 25.

Julian is now an important part of my operation. He started giving me some jumping help a couple of years ago and now works here full-time. He's a fantastic person to jump a horse – he's got a great eye and excellent balance, and rides all my young ones.

MALLARDS TREAT

Hickstead &
Gatcombe, 2002

Mallards Treat was sent to me in early 2001 when the Foot & Mouth Disease outbreak was underway which put a stop to the first half of the eventing season.

The French rider Franck Bourny had won Punchestown and Blenheim three-stars on him, but the horse was fragile and had broken down a couple of times. He was a lovely mover and jumper with a very good mind, although he looked a bit pony-ish. I suggested taking him to Kentucky for the four-star that spring because there was no eventing in Britain, and his owner Raymond Carroll thought it was a great idea.

Because of foot and mouth restrictions, it had been difficult to go galloping, let alone cross-country schooling. I did manage one schooling session and treated it like a real event, marking out the distance and riding at a proper speed.

Over in Kentucky, we led after dressage and Mallards Treat felt like a machine across country, even though it was his first four-star. He was a credit to Franck, and we finished inside the time and held our lead.

However, it wasn't quite the fairy-tale it looked like it might be because we had two showjumps down and a couple of time-faults and ended up fourth. Perhaps we were both a bit ring-rusty, having not been to any competitions that year. It was disappointing and one I should have won, for sure.

Apart from that, most places he ran he won, but he was very fragile and we only did a handful of events together in 2½ years, with me targeting the important competitions. In 2002, we had an amazing – and lucrative – week where we won the Eventing Grand Prix at Hickstead (left) and the Open Championship at Gatcombe (below) in the space of five days.

But then he injured himself again, had more time off and surgery, and when I brought him out at Weston Park the following spring he didn't feel right. I said that I didn't want to take him to Badminton because I didn't think he'd be able to finish there, so Raymond sent him to Matthew Wright to ride.

CLIMB THE HEIGHTS

Gatcombe, 2002

I BOUGHT CLIMB THE HEIGHTS out of the Doncaster Horses-In-Training Sale. The formguide *Timeform* said he was disobedient in the parade ring and at the start, and in fact he was quite naughty about doing most things. However none of that mattered once I jumped him – he could really operate and was very sharp and neat with his legs, as well as being a good mover.

He won most of his novice events as a five-year-old and he was one I thought could be a real star. For a Flat-bred horse he was a strong type and brave. As a nine-year-old he was second at the two-star at Compiègne in France and ninth at the Achselschwang three-star in Germany within six weeks.

Climb The Heights won two advanced classes and was eighth at Saumur the following year, 2002, but at Burghley he jumped into the Trout Hatchery and, after a stride, knuckled over and stuck his head right under the water. He came up and jumped the next fence, but I was in two minds about pulling him up because he didn't feel right. We kept going, but at the last water complex – where we had to jump a bridge fence under the Lion Bridge itself – I went to go the long route but we got no stride to it. He stopped and I plopped over his head and found myself sitting on the bridge.

After that he was sold to the Italian Corky Gardini, who had stopped competing for a few years, to get her going again at a lower level. She also bought New York. Stefano Brecciaroli, a leading Italian rider who has become a close friend of mine, also rode Climb The Heights a bit and won a few classes on him.

He's a horse who if I had now I'd campaign him differently and look after him more, because he had all the potential to be a really top horse. Like Splendid Style, he was a rare type of thoroughbred who had the movement and the jump.

DUDDLES

Gatcombe, 2002

DUDDLES WAS ONE OF THE LAST New Zealand thoroughbreds I brought over. He'd run in a trial race in New Zealand and wasn't fast enough, so my brother John bought him. I went over to compete at Puhinui at the end of 1998 and saw him when he'd just turned four. Duddles was a big horse with lovely, rhythmic paces and was clearly too laid-back to be a racehorse so I brought him back with another thoroughbred, Astronave. Rosemary Barlow wanted a young horse so I sold Duddles to her.

He was consistent and progressed up the grades quickly, finishing second in the one-star at Blair Castle as a six-year-old and sixth at Le Lion d'Angers three-star the following year. For a couple of years he had made a noise when he galloped, but at Pau in 2002 – where he was second in the three-star – a few vets heard him doing it on the steeplechase and after the second one told me I needed to get something done about it, he had a wind operation.

Duddles never made the noise again and was well-placed in a couple of four-stars, but he also was never quite the same again, particularly in the first year after the operation was done.

I think event horses can be better off having a bit less oxygen in their lungs and carrying on in the way that they are used to and have adapted to. Jumps help horses gallop for long distances because they take a deep breath before each one. I think at Badminton in 2014, when a lot of horses got very tired around the Huntsman's Close area, it may have been partly due to the fact that it's nearly a minute from the Lake up to Huntsman's Close without a jump, so they haven't had the opportunity to take a really deep breath and then there are three fences in very quick succession. For the first year after Duddles' operation, every time we galloped for a long distance between fences then came to a jump, he would make a horrendous mistake.

THE ARRIVAL OF THE SPANISH ARMADA

AROUND THIS TIME, I took a long, hard look at the situation I was in and the horsepower I had. I considered stopping eventing and going into the National Hunt world, but decided instead to take a different approach to the sport. I wanted more control over the horses I rode, and so started selecting and buying a very smart type of young horse I could produce from the start and sell to my owners.

It is now well-known that many of the horses I ride are Spanish-bred, which is virtually unheard-of outside Spain. They now come from three sources – Ramon Beca, his sister Ana and, more recently, my showjumping trainer Luis Àlvarez Cervera – but it all started with Fenicio.

FENICIO

World Equestrian Games in Jerez, 2002

THIS WAS ONE OF THE LAST REALLY LONG and big four-star championship cross-country courses, more than 12 minutes, and my stirrup iron smashed in half at about the 3min mark.

It was definitely Fenicio's biggest test to date. He had had lots of top placings at three-star level, but this was his first four-star. I used to break quite a lot of stirrup leathers on him because he would land quite steeply after fences, which made me slam my weight down through my feet, but this time it was the actual iron. It had happened at Fenicio's first two-star at Windsor as well, where he'd finished second, so at least he was used to it!

I tried sticking my foot into the loop of the stirrup leather, but that made me lop-sided, so I thought it was best to leave it and just carry on. It was quite a long way to go with one stirrup! But we were clear with the second fastest time of the day – the only rider quicker was the experienced Frenchman Jean Teulère, who ended up winning the individual title.

Fenicio was a lovely horse, really classy, and my first introduction to Spanish-bred horses. He came to me to be prepared for Ramon Beca, a very successful Spanish businessman who evented and also bred horses at his home near Seville. Ramon rode at several championships, including two Olympics, and he kept the horse he rode at the Sydney Olympics and the 1998 World Equestrian Games with me. Ramon, who owned and bred Fenicio, tried riding him a couple of times but the horse just had a bit too much jump; he was quite a careful, deliberate jumper who was difficult for Ramon to sit on over cross-country fences. So I got the ride and took him to Jerez when he was only nine, where he finished ninth individually, and the New Zealand team fifth. He also went to Badminton twice, in 2003 and 2005, and finished second in the World Cup Final in Pau in 2003.

MR SMIFFY

Burghley, 2003

In 2001, THE YEAR AFTER WE WON, I took Mr Smiffy back to Burghley. We led after dressage and cross-country, but had one fence down in the showjumping. It was the year that they were trialling the Olympic format of two rounds of showjumping, as an alternative to running two separate competitions for teams and individuals. One pole down in the first round dropped us to third, but jumping clear in the second round pushed us back up to second behind Blyth Tait and Ready Teddy.

Because Mr Smiffy wasn't a supple horse, you had to compromise on distances in combinations. Luckily I've never had a cross-country lesson in my life – I've learnt from falling off – and therefore have never felt that you have to fix a stride and stick to it; you can adapt on the way.

People watching me ride horses like Mr Smiffy might think I am just galloping at a fence. I know I've got the strength to do something about it in the last stride, but the horse doesn't know that and begins to think for himself and help himself, even though I'm always there to ensure it does go right. A lot of riders spend too much time setting up for a fence and taking the horse's attention away from what he is doing – and then kicking them into it.

Mr Smiffy was placed at Badminton in 2002, 2003 and 2004, but he got very careless with me in the showjumping ring, and I suggested to the owners that they put someone else on him. I assured them he'd go well across country for anyone, so J-P Sheffield got him back and did well with him.

FENICIO

Athens Olympics, 2004

I FELL OFF SHORTLY AFTER THIS PHOTO WAS TAKEN, a couple of fences before the end of the course. Athens didn't really feel like an Olympics. The equestrian competition was sited well away from the rest of the Games. Like many people, I thought the cross-country course, which went up and down a narrow strip of grass, was far too small, but it proved far too big for me!

Fenicio's real legacy was that he was the first of the Spanish horses which have formed a large part of my string in recent years. His sire, Fines, was bred from beautiful, classic Flat racing lines and had raced in Spain. His mother, Berganza, was a half-German warmblood showjumping mare. Fenicio had three full-brothers – Armada, Oplitas and Nereo, all of whom got to top level with me.

Where they are all bred in Spain is so dry at certain times of the year that you wouldn't believe you could raise horses there. It was under the sea centuries ago and there's a high salt and mineral content in the land and therefore the grass. I've often wondered if that had something to do with how very tough they all are.

LORD
KILLINGHURST

World Equestrian
Games in Aachen, 2006

British rider Owen Moore produced Lord Killinghurst, and I'd said to him a few times that if he got sick of riding the horse, I'd have a go because he looked easy! Owen pointed that I'd only seen him warm up and do dressage... He was right.

At the beginning of 2001 Owen rang me and said he was backing off from competing for a while, and asked if I wanted Lord Killinghurst. I jumped at the idea and the horse arrived the following day. Three days later I rang his owner, Nicky Salmon, to tell her the horse was settling in very well. She didn't know I'd got him! But she and her husband Robin came over and saw me and were happy for me to take over.

Very sportingly, they let me take him to Kentucky with Mallards Treat in 2001, but he damaged a tendon on the cross-country and had two years off after that.

We started again in 2003 and I realised what Owen had meant. Lord Killinghurst gave you a strange feeling, as if you were going to go under the jump, not over it. Taking him straight to a four-star probably helped, because I didn't have a chance to "fix" the problem; I just had to ride him like he was and adapt to his way of going. He felt like he had no power over a jump and got over simply on technique; he'd slither over everything, but he knew how to deal with every type of fence and he loved doing the job.

Early on in 2003 he had pretty much every showjump down at Chatsworth in a horrendous round, but I fiddled around with different ways to jump him and by Luhmühlen a month later we were hitting the same wavelength and he finished fourth. He was never a brilliant showjumper, but I worked out that I had to keep mixing it up and doing things to keep him interested and trying. He didn't have a big engine, but was nippy and very clever at pacing himself.

This picture shows him as fourth to go for the New Zealand team at the World Equestrian Games in Aachen, where we had a run-out across country. His Badminton and Burghley record, however, was extremely consistent. He gave me what is still my best Badminton placing – second – in horrendous weather conditions in 2004, and was fourth and fifth there too, as well finishing third twice and fourth at Burghley. He finished his career with just short of 2,000 British Eventing points and was a prolific winner for me.

HENRY
TANKERVILLE

Bramham, 2006

I WAS AT CAROLYN BATES' STUD ONE DAY, and she suggested I took this horse with me and tried him. He was six, only just broken, and looked as if he should be pulling a cart. But I did take him home, where I found I couldn't turn him and couldn't make him canter. However, when I trotted him to a fence, he would jump the top of the wings over a pole 18in high. I thought he might make a showjumper and bought him – very cheaply – from Carolyn. It took me a while to get him to canter a circle, and you always felt as if you were out of control.

He was a careful jumper and could jump a very big fence, but his technique wasn't quite good enough for the pure showjumpers to buy him. I took him on the lorry to a couple of events and rode him round, and when Mark Chamberlayne, who had Astronave with me, said he wanted another horse, I sold him to him and his brother Simon and they named him Henry Tankerville.

Henry kept surprising me. He wasn't the most natural galloper, but he got the hang of grinding it out. He became very consistent and won a lot, considering he looked nothing like an event horse.

He was the first horse to break my run of being in the lead after the dressage at a three-day event and failing to hold on to it when he won at the two-star Compiègne in 2004. This picture shows him winning Bramham in 2006.

We had a good relationship. I'd finish the cross-country huffing and puffing more than he was; he'd waste time at every fence because he jumped so high, so I was forever kicking him on.

In 2006, he did very well to finish the cross-country at Burghley with just 11.2 time-faults, considering how hilly and twisty it is there and also the fact that he'd fallen three weeks before at Hartpury when I thought he had broken his neck. He jumped immaculately all the way at Burghley and couldn't have gone any faster. In 2007, he was also clear inside the time at Badminton – which, being flatter, suited him better – and finished eighth.

Horses like Henry give me a lot of satisfaction. You know they aren't natural event horses, yet you've had them from the beginning and you've developed them into one.

AVEBURY

Gatcombe, 2006

This is Wiggy winning a novice on Avebury at Gatcombe in 2006. I don't remember exactly when Wiggy and I first met, but our paths crossed when competing in the late 1990s. At the time I was married to Jayne and she to William Fox-Pitt. There was an undeniably strong attraction between us and, despite our best intentions, the relationship developed. This inevitably led to the end of both our marriages around 2000/2001. It was a difficult time for all involved, being much publicised and talked about.

I only rode Avebury for a couple of weeks after breaking him in before selling him to a friend of Wiggy's, Nicola Smith, who wanted to showjump him. She jumped him as a five-year-old but then wanted to sell him to upgrade to a proper jumping type, so Wiggy bought him back. She started riding him and did well on him at novice level when he was a six-year-old.

Rosemary Barlow wanted a new horse, so I said to her that I thought I knew of one... Wiggy went away for a few days, so I sneaked him up to the gallops to see what he could do. I was quite impressed, so I suggested that Rosemary bought him for me to ride.

Avebury was quite cheeky as a young horse, and can still be naughty – he'll whip the rope out of your hands when you turn him out and he's always been a bugger to catch. But he's always felt lovely to ride. He's got a very correct technique over a fence and a balanced way of going.

He's had the occasional run-out, and that's partly his slightly disobedient nature. I got through that stage by learning not to fall for it – he'd threaten to run out one way, wait for me to correct him, and then dodge the other way.

He has won at every level, nationally and internationally, which is exceptionally rare: the one-star at Tattersalls in 2007, the two-star at the same Irish venue in 2008, and then Saumur's three-star in 2009, going inside the optimum time across country despite taking two long routes. And, of course, Burghley – twice. He doesn't look like a speed horse, but he's got a great engine and is very efficient in his stride and his movement.

DETROIT CITY

2006

I WENT TO RIDE THE PHILIP HOBBS-trained hurdler Detroit City in the winter of 2006 for a *Horse & Hound* feature about riders swapping disciplines. He was one of three top racehorses I rode over the years for the magazine – I'd also ridden the steeplechaser Teeton Mill, and I rode Mon Mome after he won his Grand National.

Both Teeton Mill and Mon Mome felt very ordinary until they had to go fast, and then they felt as though they were going up the gears effortlessly. Neither were big, impressive horses, but Detroit City, who had won the Triumph Hurdle the previous March as well the Cesarewitch that autumn, was powerful with bigger shoulders and felt as if he took a much longer stride. I loved riding all three of

them – I really enjoy National Hunt racing and the people in it and have made a few forays into buying and selling National Hunt store horses.

I've ridden another Grand National winner as well. When I was at Roger Stack's yard, Lord Onslow brought his hunter, an ex-racehorse, to me because he wouldn't jump hedges with him. When I rode him, he jumped a pole like he'd showjumped all his life – he was beautiful to ride and a lovely, intelligent horse. I jumped everything I could on him for two weeks and loved him, and when Lord Onslow came to collect him I asked him who the horse was. It was Hallo Dandy, who had won the 1984 National.

SILBURY HILL

Burghley, 2007

THIS FENCE IN THE MAIN ARENA was very near the end of the track. Silbury Hill was starting to run out of gas and we came off the turn to this on a half-stride and just got it all wrong. It was a shame because he'd gone very well up to that point.

Silbury Hill, like Avebury, was named after ancient earthworks near where I live in Wiltshire. He was bred by Jane Davies out of Dawdle and Gumley's full-sister, Waddle, by Maximillian Saluut, and was owned by Paul Ridgeon. He was a horse with enormous promise who had won the last running of Punchestown that May. The following spring he went to Badminton and felt perfect all the way until the road crossing two fences from the finish. As

he galloped across the road, I thought he'd broken a leg because something felt very wrong. But because we were so near the jump, which he'd spotted, I couldn't do anything about it. He towed me to it and actually he felt fine in those last few strides. We had no alternative but to jump the fence, and I pulled up and jumped off as soon as he landed. His legs looked fine and he walked and trotted up sound but it turned out that he'd pretty much ruptured a front tendon.

He did recover, however, and went to Bridget and Katie Parker to help teach modern pentathletes about the showjumping phases of their sport.

GINGER MAY KILLINGHURST

Chatsworth, 2008

The Bermudan rider MJ Tumbridge had been round Badminton on Ginger May Killinghurst, who was a half-sister to Lord Killinghurst but by a warmblood dressage sire instead of a thoroughbred. When she gave up eventing at the top level, MJ suggested the owner, John Studd, rang me, and he sent her to me in 2007.

She was a nice mare who did a good test and MJ had done a great job with her, but the one thing she wasn't was a Ferrari. I started to ride her with more speed than MJ had done, which Ginger May took well – but she wanted me to slow down at each fence.

I tipped her up at the third fence at Bramham. I was making a conscious effort to keep her moving up to each fence so she got the hang of keeping going forward until I said not to and she stood off it a stride early and was already coming down when she reached the fence. She only just made the front rail of the oxer!

However, I took her to Pau, where she was clear inside the time around the four-star track. She gave me 100% but she was very tired in the showjumping the next day and had several fences down, although she still finished sixth. She slept for about two weeks when we got home! After Chatsworth, where this picture was taken, I told the owners they should accept that she wasn't going to be properly competitive at four-star and she went to stud, although she did give British rider Laura Collett her first spin round Burghley in 2010. Both Ginger May and Lord Killinghurst were very genuine in their attitudes, which is another example of a trait being passed down from a dam.

LORD
KILLINGHURST

Hong Kong Olympics,
2008

THE CROSS-COUNTRY AT THE 2008 OLYMPICS gave me possibly the most exciting eight minutes of my life. I've never gone so fast nor taken so many chances.

At the first competitor briefing, we learned that the course was two minutes shorter than had been advertised. The New Zealand team had been led to believe it was 11½ minutes because officials wanted us to get our horses very fit to cope with the humidity of Hong Kong in August. I thought that could actually play to my advantage: lots of jumping efforts in a short space of time would make it extremely difficult to get the time.

Lord Killinghurst's weak link was the showjumping and, with two rounds ahead of us, I asked the rest of the team – Mark Todd, Caroline Powell, Joe Meyer and Heelan Tompkins – if they were happy for me to live life on the edge. My plan was to have three rails in hand going into the showjumping, which I knew I'd need to be able to win.

The New Zealand way of thinking has always been that if we get three great individual results, we will win a team medal. We were always encouraged to try to win individual medals, rather than ride with the team in mind, which suits our characters.

Before I went cross-country, I watched some of the good, fast riders and saw that they were already 10 seconds down by the first minute marker. So I didn't warm up very much – with the heat and humidity I didn't want to waste any of his energy – and I left the start-box faster than I've ever done, going practically flat out to the first fence. Whenever I couldn't see a stride

I kicked, and each time Lord Killinghurst found more. Every time I thought I should do one more stride, I kicked and thought to myself that I'd saved a quarter of a second. I was right on my minute markers and, although the horse felt a bit shocked, he happily went along with it. I did think "This feels crazily fast", but it was very exciting.

Looking back, I'm positive Lord Killinghurst would gone inside the time. He still had pace left and it was downhill from the second last fence to the last. But, stupidly, I slowed down a bit; the second last was a double of angled brushes and the fence before that was a simple house, which was so small and innocuous that I thought I should slow up to avoid taking a "flyer" over that and being out of shape when turning to the brushes.

So we popped over the house but it felt like he'd lost concentration, being asked to steady after such a forward, positive round. The momentum went and it felt like there was no distance to the brushes. He did well to jump the first of them, and then I literally lifted him up and put him down over the second one, but it had a little ditch on the landing side and he slipped his front feet into it and knuckled over.

I shouldn't have altered the rhythm we had because it suddenly changed the whole feeling for him, but I don't regret it. Coming home clear with 10 time-faults wouldn't have won us a medal, and that's what Olympics are about. I was furious with myself, and it was so frustrating when I could see the finish flags ahead of me, but I'd do it again in a heartbeat.

AVEBURY

Express Eventing at Cardiff, 2008

THIS NEW COMPETITION WAS A TOTAL COCK-UP. Top eventers were invited to compete for fantastic prize-money and that, combined with the thought of packing the Millennium Stadium in Cardiff with spectators, was exciting – in theory. The format of dressage to music with 'Strictly Come Dancing'-style judging and then showjumping and indoor "cross-country" was gimmicky, but we went along with it.

The nearer the event came, the more obvious it became that very few tickets had been sold. And we heard chat from the "guinea pig" riders they'd got to test it that the surface was very slippery. Whenever I watched a rugby match from there I noticed that the backs often slipped for no reason.

But the organisers assured us it would be fine, and we turned up at the crack of dawn on a freezing cold day to see the venue and the course that we would be tackling later that day. We became concerned when we realised that you could hardly tell there had been a rugby match on the ground the day before, because it was on a false surface, and started to realise it really was going to be slippery. It was cold and the stadium was pretty empty.

I thought Pierre Michelet, the French course-designer, had done a good job, but as soon as we started you could see the horses trying to keep on their feet, sliding, losing confidence and back-pedalling. Several riders lost their way and many horses became frenetic during the timed "pit-stop" in which we had to change kit before going cross-country.

Mary King's Olympic horse Call Again Cavalier broke a leg in full view of the spectators, and it wasn't fun to see other good horses struggling. Avebury was eight and young to be doing it, and the further we went round the more he was telling me "No, thank you" and we didn't finish.

It was full credit to Oliver Townend, who won by miles on Flint Curtis and took home the £100,000. The competition was potentially a very good idea and it was a good venue, but it didn't work, the ground was dangerous for horses and it was a big opportunity lost for the sport.

EPIC

Bramham, 2009

AVEBURY WAS THE THIRD FOAL I had out of Memento and the only one foaled at home. My daughters Melissa and Rebecca named him Buddy, which has stuck as his stable name. When he was due to be weaned, I collected another foal from Carolyn Bates to keep him company. She gave him to me, and he turned out to be Epic. We ran them together for three years before I broke them in.

Libby Sellar bought Epic when he was a young horse. He was a classy individual who got to advanced level very easily – it took Avebury a couple of years to catch up with him. Epic's weak bit was the showjumping, but he was really good on the flat and on the cross-country. He had soundness problems, though, and he went to a Pony Club lad to have fun with, ending up giving him experience at intermediate level eventing.

OPLITAS

Weston Park, 2010

THIS IS OPLITAS FINISHING SECOND to Mr Cruise Control in an advanced section. It was a pretty successful day: I took five advanced horses, and won all three advanced classes and finished second to myself in two of them!

Oplitas is a full-brother to Armada and Nereo. They are all a little bit odd, and in some ways he is the oddest. None of them liked being shod or clipped to begin with and he was the worst. When he was broken in, he bucked every time you touched him with the leg. But he felt very talented, and was highly successful for a horse who was so tricky to ride for the first five minutes that you were on him. Like Armada, I always felt I was a little strong for him.

It got to the stage where, when he was an intermediate horse, I got the talented British rider Piggy French, who was looking for horses at the time, to come and try him. I rode him first, then popped her on and he went very well for her. I was very tempted to let her take him to ride for a while, but the fact that I knew he was so difficult when you first got on made both she and I nervous I think, and I carried on with him.

He won an advanced class at Belton when he was eight and one at Withington the following season. Then at the beginning of 2012 my friend Stefano Brecciaroli, who only had one horse, wasn't confident that he'd got enough FEI points to fulfil the Olympic criteria if the Italians didn't qualify a team for London, so I suggested he had Oplitas for the year to try and get some points. He rode him in some three-stars and got good placings, and therefore points, and became attached to him.

Stefano isn't as tall as me nor so strong with his legs, and I was amazed when I saw them together after a couple of months – they'd really clicked. We eventually sold him to another Italian rider, Giovanni Ugolotti, who's still got him.

ARMADA

Badminton, 2010

I FIRST SAW ARMADA WHEN HE WAS THREE at Ramon Beca's farm near Seville. He was very big and gangly, so they left him a while before breaking him in, and he came over to me when he'd just turned five. The moment I sat on him, I knew he was very powerful but also light in the hand. When he was broken in, they'd said they couldn't really canter him as his stride was just too big for the school, but he learnt very quickly – he's very intelligent. He was always very brave and I knew he'd be an unbelievable cross-country horse. He was the first horse I sold Paul Ridgeon, who had owned Wiggy's four-star horse, Willy B Free.

Riding Armada across country was not like riding a normal horse. He was so brave and clever with his feet that you never felt as if you were doing more than schooling round a pre-novice. He was third at Punchestown and Blenheim when only an eight-year-old, and fourth at Bramham and eighth at Burghley the following year aged nine. He went clear across country at seven out of the nine four-stars we did together and no horse has ever made it feel so easy

Never did you feel you needed to add any power or wake him up. At the top-level events I don't remember wearing spurs or carrying a whip, even round the biggest tracks. His adjustability is amazing; he could do two less strides in a combination than any other horse, or add in as many as you like. You could change your mind at the last minute and he'd instantly respond but you had to go with him. His brothers are perhaps not as naturally gifted, but because they don't quite have the range of stride he has, they are easier to train.

ARMADA

Burghley, 2009

ARMADA HAD NEVER REARED UP during a dressage test until Badminton in 2009, when it was blowing a gale during our test and he saw a tent on the edge of the arena fly up in front of him during the halt. He went to run backwards, and I kept my leg on to say "wait", and he got himself in a bit of a temper and stood up. He didn't do it again until Burghley that autumn when he did it again at exactly the same place in the test. He felt like he got up very high – and when he came down he'd leap forward and only just land inside the boards! This didn't do our marks any good, which is a shame as he is such a talented horse.

Eventually the cross-country started feeling too easy and too small for him as well – if ever a horse needed a five-star event it was Armada. I think somehow I just knew him too well and was a bit too strong in my legs for him. Sometimes a different rider and a change of scene can help an experienced horse be competitive again, and I suggested he went to Oliver Townend.

Oliver, who is a friend of mine, is one of the most talented riders there is – not only does he have a very competitive attitude, but he has excellent hand-eye-leg co-ordination, and I thought they might work well together. Armada's owner Paul Ridgeon agreed, and Oliver was very excited to try the horse. It's worked well for all of us – Oliver was second at Badminton on Armada in 2014, and Paul has since had three more horses with me.

AVEBURY

Pau, 2009

I let Avebury down in a major way here. It was his first four-star when he was only nine and he did a lovely dressage test to sit just a few marks behind the leaders. I thought Pau would be easy for him because it's flat, and because he's polite to ride we would be able to nip around its tight bends.

We'd done all the difficult bits of the cross-country and there wasn't much left to jump when we got to the final water. I admit I was counting the money! We had to jump down into the water before curving right to jump up the step out and then it was a couple of strides to another simple fence. He jumped in very well, but I turned far too sharply before the step and came to it on a half-stride. He was a mile away from it and tried to come up, but didn't make

it and we were fired into the bank. One minute I was thinking how well it was all going, and the next we'd smacked into the ground. Luckily, he was absolutely fine.

The following year, 2010, he ducked out of skinny fences at both Badminton and Burghley. At Badminton, he shied at someone's dog and I've learnt that if he shies, it means I'm not going fast enough. He's a clever little monkey and if I ride him like I've stolen him, he's unbelievable but it's more difficult now he's older and knows so much about the sport. At Burghley he dived off a straightforward corner at the bottom of the Dairy Mound. After that I started playing around with him and if he shied, I'd give him a pat – basically doing the opposite of what he expected me to do.

ARMADA,

Tattersalls, 2010

THIS WAS A PREP RUN FOR THE FOUR-STAR at Luhmühlen, so I'd planned on going quietly and we were galloping round, happy as Larry. He jumped into the water fine, but somehow I let go of the reins, which flicked straight over his head. Without any guidance from on top, he locked on to a rock garden which was part of the decoration on the way out of the water, jumped that and I found myself heading back round the course the way we had come – with no reins.

By this time, the technical delegate, Giuseppe Della Chiesa, was in hot pursuit, showing an impressive turn of foot. I was trying quietly to grasp the bridle, but the more I moved in the saddle the faster Armada went. Eventually I got hold of his cheek-piece and pulled him up, got the reins back over his head, turned round and set off again. We got 20 penalties for jumping an "alternative" route out of the water, but we did finish!

LUHMÜHLEN

2010

HERE'S STEFANO BRECCIAROLI ACTING as chauffeur! Stefano is one of my best friends in the sport and godfather to both my younger children, Lily and Zach. We've had various dealings in horses together over the years, and he came to stay with me to prepare for the London Olympics in 2012. He's been on the Italian eventing team lots of times, but had really caught the British media's eye with a superb dressage test for second place at that stage at the World Equestrian Games in 2010 at Kentucky. However, his horse, Apollo, is pure warmblood and got a lot of time-penalties across country at Kentucky, so it was my job to get the pair of them really fit before the Olympics in London.

NEREO

Eridge, 2005

I loved Nereo from the moment he arrived as a four-year-old, despite that fact that he was as ugly as can be. His brothers had elegance, but he was a funny shape with a short neck and a very powerful way of doing things. Luckily, I managed to sell him to Libby Sellar over the phone while she was in New Zealand before she had the chance to see him!

The dressage judges couldn't see what I was feeling in the early days either, but he won a novice class at Barbury as a five-year-old and a couple of good riders told me what a good galloper he was after watching him across country and this is luckily what Libby remembers seeing in the beginning. Now he has grown into himself and we think he's very handsome. He has always been very suspicious of anything that is at all different, but he's totally genuine at the same time. This picture was taken at Eridge, during his first season eventing. He was five years old and picked up his first British Eventing points by jumping clear – his first – and coming third.

NEREO

Aachen, 2010

In 2010 I was weighing up my options for the World Equestrian Games that autumn. I'd been to Aachen in Germany, which is basically Europe's most prestigious show, with Avebury the year before and got the fastest time across country despite taking a long route at a tricky corner. The New Zealand federation likes to use Aachen as a trial run before a championship because it's a particularly high-pressure place to ride. Competing alongside showjumping and dressage legends in front of a vast, extremely knowledgeable crowd is great practice for a championship atmosphere and I always find it inspiring to be there.

I said to my federation that I wanted to take Nereo and to use it as a proper event and not pussyfoot around. He started off the cross-country fast and went round miles quicker than anyone else – and did it effortlessly. I became the first non-German to win the eventing competition at Aachen, and it's pretty cool to look up at the list of winners in each discipline which are engraved on to the side of the main stadium and see my name there, and be the proud owner of the Aachen green jacket given to all major winners at the show over the years.

Nereo had answered all my questions. He was 10 by now and had won Bramham the year before and finished 11th at Badminton with a double clear, and so he was the obvious choice for the WEG.

NEREO

World Equestrian
Games in Kentucky,
2010

IT FELT GREAT TO BE PART OF A NEW ZEALAND team that was on the up again. A lot of people didn't give us much hope of a medal, but I enjoyed my role in rejuvenating the team and acting as team captain. Suddenly we had a bunch of riders who wanted to win the competition, rather than just get their national caps. Mark Todd was a vital part of that. His attitude rubs off on all of us and makes us all raise our game.

After that Aachen win I thought I had a chance of a medal, but I hadn't been to Lexington for a few years and thought the course would probably be very big. Now that I've been back a few times since, I think the terrain – which walks very undulating but rides fast – and the perfect ground helps horses gallop. For Nereo to go round the cross-country as easily as he did under the optimum time was a bit of a surprise.

But I must be losing my edge – look back at the picture on page 52 of me at the Barcelona Olympics. Back then I was good enough to take both hands of the reins; now I can only do it with one! Curiously, there's a picture of me in exactly the same one-handed pose jumping into the water on Quimbo at the annual four-star event at Kentucky when we won there in 2013.

The Germans, who had led after dressage, were wiped out on the cross-country and our team of (left to right) Clark Johnstone (Orient Express), Caroline Powell (Mac Macdonald), Mark Todd (Grass Valley) and me vaulted up the order towards the medals. I was in fifth place individually after cross-country, and when I saw there were a couple of weaker showjumpers in front of me, I quietly thought to myself that I could make it up to a medal position.

Nereo jumped a lovely clear and we ended up clinching both the team bronze and an individual bronze medal behind Germany's Michael Jung and Britain's William Fox-Pitt. To win the medals in the showjumping was particularly pleasing; I felt I'd come a long way since that Barcelona disaster back in 1992. It was my first individual medal and I enjoyed standing on the podium in my own right for once.

MR CRUISE CONTROL

Hartpury, 2011

In 2005, Nicky and Robin Salmon said they wanted a young horse, and the only one I had available was Oplitas. I wasn't convinced he was the right one for them at that time, so I said that if they saw something they liked, I'd come and have a look. They got me to come and try a four-year-old by the Irish jumping stallion Cruising who was doing the Burghley Young Event Horse qualifier at Gatcombe with Jayne Wilson.

Mr Cruise Control was big, but nowhere near as big as he is now! Three riders were watching me ride him, and they all said I couldn't believe I was trying him. But I had a feeling he'd be OK. He felt rhythmic and trainable, and he came to me that autumn.

Mr Cruise Control is nothing like any of the other horses I've got. He grew and grew and grew – and he was slow. Really slow. When I started taking him to the gallops, I could have got off and walked beside him. A lot of horses would have objected to the grinding he had to do to get up the gallops, but he's a real trier and his mind is in the right place. He's always been a jumper and his technique got better and better as he got older and stronger.

He was a bit quirky when he started – he once whipped round with me between fences at a novice event and I nearly fell off, which isn't something that happens with many of my five-year-olds. But he went up through the grades quickly, and won an intermediate and a one-star competition as a six-year-old. He's at least 17.2hh, and one hell of a big unit. But on a flat surface he has a very easy gallop stride.

There were a few hiccups at the big events early on because I would try to organise the distance to the jump. I was trying to be too helpful because he was weak and immature, but he could shut down on you very quickly for a big horse. Suddenly the distance would be gone and he'd run out.

But he got the hang of things, and in 2010 he was fourth and ninth in his first two four-stars, Luhmühlen and Pau – and he was still only nine.

In 2011 he won the international class at Hartpury for the second year running, and he finished second at Pau at the end of the season.

CALICO JOE

Blair Castle, 2011

I bought Calico Joe as an unbroken three-year-old. It was at a time when I was thinking of shifting my career towards buying National Hunt store horses, breaking them in, and selling them to the trainers when they were ready to run. I'd always liked thoroughbreds and the bloodstock industry and went to some Flat breeze-up sales at Doncaster to have a look, quickly realising it took an awful lot of money to play at that game. The National Hunt world was more realistic, but again I realised soon on that I had to buy horses I liked the look of, regardless of pedigree, as I couldn't afford the ones with smart bloodlines. If they weren't good enough to race, I thought I could turn them into eventers.

Alfie Buller, the former Irish Olympic eventer and an old friend of mine, encouraged me. I knew he had a backlog of horses from his Scarvagh House Stud in Northern Ireland and, as soon as I told him what I was planning, a lorry-load of 14 three-year-olds arrived. I got them working; they all sold and most of them won. So I bought another batch of 14 from Alfie, and Calico Joe was among them. He was one of the best up the gallops, but every fourth time he worked he'd tie up. My main customer then was the Grand National-winning trainer Nigel Twiston-Davies – I'd take them up to his yard in the Cotswolds and he'd say which ones he liked – and although he was quite keen to keep Calico Joe, I told him about the tying up, for which I couldn't find a reason.

Joe was always a nice looker but didn't feel that great over a fence. He also weaves, wind-sucks and box-walks... I thought I'd do a few events on him and sell him as a novice. He was petrified of coloured jumps and of the cross-country, although I reckoned if I went fast enough he'd have to jump! Luis Àlvarez de Cervera, who is our team jumping trainer, got on him one day at home and soon hopped off pretty smartly, telling me I was mad even to attempt to jump a fixed fence on him.

Calico Joe felt like he had no belief in himself over a fence. He'd feel as if he was going to stop at the first three or four fences – he didn't, but neither did he get very high over them. He never felt brave cross-country but he got used to doing it, and it's not as though I beat him over them or anything; he's got enough problems without being scared of me as well. He got to advanced level without hardly ever jumping a clear round in the showjumping.

He had six months off at the beginning of 2011 and when he came back into work I kept putting off jumping him, as I hadn't exactly missed it! Eventually I entered him somewhere and thought I really had better jump him first. For the first time, he actually felt like he could do it, and I thought maybe the penny had dropped.

His next event was the advanced at Gatcombe – and he jumped clear and won. I took him to Blair Castle where the ground was bottomless. He flew round the cross-country, but I could feel him struggling in the showjumping warm-up. But blow me down, he went clear and won!

NEREO,

Burghley, 2011

The Badminton I felt I really let slip between my fingers was the one Mark Todd won in 2011. I went into the showjumping in third place and, as Nereo had barely had a rail down in two years, I felt I was in a strong position to put pressure on the whole situation. But I was too casual and, bang, I had the second and third fences down. Toddy won and I was only 12th!

This picture, taken that year at Burghley, looks a bit hairy, but Nereo is actually on his way to second place. He's not a big fan of roofs over fences and this had an arch over it. I was behind time so going quite fast, but it didn't feel as dramatic as this looks.

NIGEL TWISTON-DAVIES

Cheltenham, 2011

About 20 years ago, I sold an owner of Nigel Twiston-Davies' a horse I'd bought out of racing in New Zealand and hoped to turn into an eventer, but it was just a bit too quick over coloured poles to be a money-spinner in that sphere. He won five or six races for them and over the years I sent a few more to Nigel.

We became friends, and when I started playing with buying and selling store horses, he was the first person to show interest in them. I started helping with the jumping of some of his horses; Fundamentalist, who had won the Royal & SunAlliance Hurdle at the Cheltenham Festival but had several falls over fences, was one of the first. It's not rocket science – you're just giving the horses a way to deal with making a mistake. Fundamentalist still made mistakes, but at least he stood up after I'd done some work with him.

I found it exciting and it's a fun environment to be in. Baby Run, who I worked with just before he won the Aintree Fox Hunter's with Nigel's younger son, Willie, dumped me as soon as he got in the school – and the lads laughed their heads off because they knew he would! Baby Run could have been an eventer; he's a beautiful jumper. I jumped up to 1m 30cm on him – in a racing saddle! Imperial Commander, whom I rode after he won the 2010 Cheltenham Gold Cup, was lovely to jump too.

In another life I'd have loved to have been a jump jockey. I read the *Racing Post* every day and take a keen interest in the sport.

It's interesting to see how racehorse training has changed since I was at Derek Kent's in the early 1980s. The standard of staff and work riders is much higher, they jump them a lot more and do considerably more with poles and in the school.

NEREO

London Olympics, 2012

Although I have competed at six Olympics, Dawdle officially started at the Sydney Games in 2000 because he passed the trot-up but went lame before the dressage – so London 2012 was really my seventh.

I went to Greenwich really feeling that this was the one.

But as soon as we got to London, events seemed to conspire against me. I'd been told for the previous six months that I would be last (generally considered the advantageous position) of the five New Zealand riders to go for the team, no matter which horse I took.

Then, after the first trot-up, I was told that I'd be winning my gold medal from the fourth, not fifth, slot – that honour was to go to Mark Todd. I've learnt there's not much point throwing your toys about, so I calmly asked the New Zealand hierarchy why that had changed, and I wasn't given an answer.

We moved on to the dressage, and as I was warming up, the heavens opened and thunder and lightning boomed and

crackled round the stadium. Nereo and I weren't bothered by it and were working in very well.

The rider before me, Sweden's Niklas Lindback, went into the arena ready to do his test and I was told I had seven minutes left to go. So I started to crank Nereo up, only to hear it announced that there was to be a delay. Niklas appeared back, looking confused, and headed towards the stables. I sent our chef d'equipe Erik Duvander to tell the organisers that no way can they stop the competition. We were told something about the roof of one of the judge's boxes coming loose and that there was definitely to be a hold. I went off to the indoor arena while they decided how long the hold was to be.

By this time, I'm soaking wet and the horse naturally thinks he has finished for the day. After a 10-minute delay I had to start warming up again and was told I had ten minutes to go until my test. The stop-start warm up and confusion unnerved Nereo, and I was wet through and slipping around on a saddle that felt like a bar of soap. We never got back to the place where we were in our work and we scored 45. The bottom line is, you plan your warm-up to produce the horse at its best for the eight minutes you are in there, and they don't have an extra 10–15 minutes to give beyond that, which is what I had to ask Nereo to do. It's pretty hard to win gold from 21st place. I was really angry and felt it was a bad decision by the ground jury and the technical delegate that was unprecedented and appallingly handled. It also kept running through my head that it shouldn't have been me in that slot in the first place.

The cross-country was how we thought it would be – a small, tight track around which the time was going to be hard to get. Our team all knew we were to go as fast as we could, and Nereo stormed round. But as we came to the flat, galloping section towards the end, I came round a corner at full speed and saw that a crossing-point steward had put a rope across the track. It was too late to do anything about it and I galloped straight through it. I thought I was going to flip over, but instead the steward must have had a serious rope burn to his hand. At this point you can't blame me for thinking, "Someone doesn't want me to win this."

The cross-country picture on the previous page sums up Greenwich. The crowds were vast and very noisy and, although the fences were beautiful, they weren't big.

As a team, we were still in fourth place after cross-country. We knew from the test event the year before that some horses didn't cope well with jumping on the platform that was used to raise the stadium well above the ground, but Nereo was happy on it. He jumped clear in the first round to help the New Zealand team move up to the bronze medal.

He jumped just as well in the second round to decide the individual placings, except that down one line I over-rode between two of the fences and he had one of them down. I finished fourth which, at an Olympics, may as well be last. You get nothing.

It was another chance lost and while I was very pleased with Nereo's performance, I was bitterly disappointed by the whole experience.

NICHOLSON FAMILY

Britain, 2012

THIS IS ME WITH MY DAUGHTERS Melissa, plus her husband Adam, Rebecca (right) and Lily (in front) at my grandson Cruz's christening. There were lots of jokes about galloping grandfathers when people found out I was one! Melissa used to be a sales rep for Toggi but is now a full-time mum with two children – her second, Bella, was born in June 2014.

Rebecca lives in London and has a great job as a business developer at MediaPlanet, which produces educational supplements for newspapers. She and I are pictured together after she graduated from Nottingham University with a first-class honours degree. Melissa and Rebecca are both doing well and I'm very proud of them.

NICHOLSON FAMILY

New Zealand, 2012

After the Olympics, we all travelled home for an official team welcome. The New Zealand High Performance people were concerned that I was only flying back for two days so I told them I had other important events coming up, and I could tell they weren't too impressed. Therefore, going on to win every single one that I'd reeled off to them gave me a very good feeling.

We spent a couple of hours in Mark Todd's home town, Cambridge, which is near where I come from too, and my family – (left to right) Helen, Jamie, Liz, John and Sarah – all came together for an hour in a pub. I'd actually forgotten to bring my Olympic medal, so I had to borrow one from other of the other competitors! It was good to go back. I rarely get time to go home and you forget how involved a whole country gets in the Olympics.

ON THE CREST
OF A WAVE

I'D PLANNED TO GO HOME FROM THE LONDON OLYMPICS with an individual gold medal. That didn't happen. But it kick-started a run of major victories that gave me the most successful 12 months of my career. It included five four-star wins and five at three-star level; a feat of which I'm very proud and one which we might not see anyone else manage for a while. It was achieved with a lovely team of horses; the nicest I have ridden.

AVEBURY

Burghley, 2012

THIS WAS MY FIRST FOUR-STAR WIN FOR 12 YEARS, since Mr Smiffy in 2000. It was Avebury's owners Rosemary and Mark Barlow's first at the highest level, and I was delighted for them as they have been incredibly loyal to me since the days of Spinning Rhombus. Avebury was second after dressage, whizzed round the cross-country and had one fence down on the last day. The American rider Sinead Halpin had been in the lead, but she hit three showjumps so we won.

After the sour taste the London Olympics had left in my mouth, it felt great to win a major competition.

QUIMBO

Boekelo, 2012

I GO TO RAMON BECA'S EVERY YEAR to look at his youngsters, and on one trip he asked me if I'd look at the horses his sister Ana breeds for showjumping. I ended up buying Quimbo and Qwanza, both by the German grand prix showjumping sire Lacros out of mares who were half-sisters – and related to Ramon's mares.

I got quite attached to Quimbo – he's beautiful to look at, and when I took him cross-country schooling he seemed to love it – and sold him to Libby Sellar. He was always a winner. I did fall off him at his first event at Stilemans when I got hung up on a tree on an island in the water jump, but he won an intermediate at the end of his first season as a five-year-old. He also won the two-star at Tattersalls in Ireland when he was seven and was third in the World Young Horse Championships at Le Lion d'Angers, fitting in an advanced win in between the two.

Quimbo is a pleasure to have – a very gentle, kind horse who the children could go and play with, he is so friendly and quiet. He won the international class at Burnham Market in 2011 but then went through a patch of bad luck that year.

However, he had a phenomenal 2012. I needed him to get a qualifying score at Saumur in France in case I needed him for the London Olympics. He ran across country at the end of a very rainy day when the ground had cut up so I didn't go fast or take any risks, but he still finished ninth. After that he was my third choice – behind Nereo and Avebury – for London.

Quimbo was second to Avebury at Barbury and then I ran him in the Eventing Grand Prix at Hickstead to add a bit of speed into his bag of tricks and he was second behind the Irish showjumper Trevor Breen, who was riding a grand prix jumping horse.

Quimbo then won Blenheim's young horse class – and then took Boekelo a month later. It was nice to beat Michael Jung – who'd just made history by being Olympic, World and European Champion simultaneously through taking gold in London – in the showjumping. I was in second place going into the final phase and jumped clear while he had two down, which felt quite sweet. I then took Nereo to Pau and the same thing happened!

NEREO

Pau, 2012

Because Nereo didn't go to Badminton in the spring (as it was cancelled) and had come out of London so well, I took him to Pau for the last four-star of the year. He was third going into the showjumping, but jumped clear to finish on his dressage score of 39.3. When Jock Paget and Michael Jung both had a fence down, Nereo won. He deserved it because he's a top, top horse. I don't think people would appreciate how good his competition record was unless they studied it.

It was extraordinary how everything fell into place that autumn. I hadn't won a four-star since Mr Smiffy's Burghley in 2000, and now I'd won two in two months, plus a couple of three-stars.

You can see in this picture that I am wearing custom-made, prescription sports eye-wear. It's taken a long time to find the solution to the fact that I have growths on the front of my corneas, which is a common problem caused by exposure to high UV light levels in the southern hemisphere. This makes my eyes sensitive to dust and wind, and also affects my vision in one eye. As a result I can't wear contact lenses on top of my corneas, and I caused quite a bit of comment when I first appeared wearing glasses to go cross-country. These "goggles" are amazing and make a big difference. I can still ride without them if I have to when it is raining, but I will be a few seconds slower on a five-minute cross-country course without them as I have to take time to judge distances.

LUIS ÀLVAREZ DE CERVERA

Kentucky, 2013

EVEN BEFORE LUIS STARTED HELPING ME with Spinning Rhombus's showjumping after the Barcelona Olympics, I'd watch him ride. He's an artist on a horse. He was the first Spaniard to compete at six Olympics – at Barcelona and Atlanta in eventing and at Munich, Montreal, Los Angeles, Seoul and Barcelona in showjumping. He's a true horseman who is interested in all elements of how a horse performs.

I now work with him mostly at competitions, although he comes to my yard perhaps six times a year for a full day and I'll jump every horse I can with him. Luis is a great believer in repetition, and since I started working with him more, I jump my young horses a lot more at home. We do a lot of exercises which are small in terms of height but using difficult stride patterns, which I do day in, day out. Like children, the younger you start doing work like that the more it sinks into their technique. You don't want them to get tired doing it though, which is why we keep the fences small.

He has also helped Mark Todd a lot, and between us we gradually weaned the rest of the New Zealand squad on to him. Luis became our team showjumping trainer in 2009 and has helped us all considerably. He's much more than just a showjumping coach – he's passionately interested in how all our horses perform in each phase. He's become a very good friend, and I'm now riding some of the horses he has bred at his base near Madrid, such as Jet Set IV.

QUIMBO

Kentucky, 2013

AFTER THAT MAGIC RUN IN 2012, eventing fans might have been rather surprised when Quimbo had a couple of run-outs at national events in the spring of 2013. But I knew I was using them to educate him – he'd got a bit full of himself and over-confident – and I wasn't worried. Having won Burghley on Avebury in September 2012, I took Quimbo to Kentucky six months later to try to put myself in line for the elusive Rolex Grand Slam bid (worth $350,000 to the rider who can win Kentucky, Badminton and Burghley consecutively). This has only been done once before, by Pippa Funnell in 2003, which shows what an achievement that was.

We were second after dressage, and I was amazed at how easy Quimbo made the cross-country feel. We took the lead overnight and were able to have a bit in hand for the showjumping. We did collect a couple of time-faults, but jumped clear for my first Kentucky victory. Suddenly, the Grand Slam was live – and so was William Fox-Pitt's, because his had been held over a year from 2012 when Badminton was cancelled. The pressure was on, and the media went mad though, luckily, they only had a week to think about it.

NEREO AND AVEBURY

Badminton, 2013

KNOWING THAT I HAD NEREO AND AVEBURY AT BADMINTON – the two horses in which I had most confidence and belief – meant I felt I was in a very strong position and could enjoy the razzmatazz that came with the double Grand Slam bid. There was a huge amount of press attention – overleaf I am talking to BBC commentator Clare Balding. From the moment I got back from Kentucky, I had endless calls from the media wanting to talk to me – especially from New Zealand.

I thought it was great for the sport. William and I were both taking two four-star winners to Badminton, and that, added to our personal history, attracted a lot of interest. But everyone forgot about the other 80 competitors! How did Michael Jung, the World, Olympic and European champion making his Badminton debut on his best horse, slip under the radar?

Michael led the dressage, which is what I expected, and the judges had William and me on level pegging, with his Parklane Hawk scoring 40 and Nereo 40.2. In the photograph on the right you can see him scoring a 10 – for the halt. On cross-country day, Avebury did his bit and went beautifully, clear and inside the time.

As I was just about to go on Nereo, William was finishing in the main arena on Parklane Hawk and as he went

through the finish he wound the crowd up, getting them cheering and clapping. As a result I couldn't hear the starter counting me down and Nereo got pretty over-excited, but that's gamesmanship and at our level we should be able to cope with that. I did something similar to William the next day before his showjumping round as a bit of payback. People who hadn't seen what had happened the day before wouldn't have understood, but he did.

Nereo was also clear inside the time across country, and William and I were third and fourth before the showjumping, with Jock Paget just ahead of us and behind Michael.

I knew I still had a good chance. Nereo jumped a great round and was clear, while William had one rail down, dropping below me. I was still in the hunt – but then Jock jumped clear, despite me willing him to have one down! My two minutes of living the dream were over, and when Michael Jung just got a bit forward running downhill into the last fence and his horse, Sam, took it out with his back legs, Jock got the title at his first attempt.

I'd given it my best shot. I was very happy with what I'd done, and you can't control other people's performances. I thoroughly enjoyed the whole week and all the hype, which is purely down to having two such nice horses to ride.

MR CRUISE CONTROL

Luhmühlen, 2013

MR CRUISE CONTROL'S BEST FOUR-STARS are Luhmühlen and Pau, because they are flat – Burghley would never be his track. He had his day in the sun at Luhmühlen and won very impressively, finishing on his dressage score of 38.

His warm-up at big events is rather different to most horses'; if you rode him in for too long you'd end up carrying him around the arena, so I get on, blast him around for a couple of minutes and go straight in. That way you can get a very elegant, focused test.

I like this picture of Mr Cruise Control because it looks as if he's trying really hard, which is him through and through. He's having time off with a tendon injury at the moment, but to be fair to him he's done very well to stay sound this long. He's done a lot for a big horse, and every time he gallops it's hard work for his heart and lungs. Amazingly, he's still excited when he gets to the gallops – I wouldn't be if I were him!

QWANZA

Luhmühlen, 2013

QWANZA, WHO BELONGS TO MARK AND ROSEMARY BARLOW, was always slightly trailing in her three-parts brother Quimbo's wake. He's big, black and handsome, and she's smaller, plainer and hotter. It took her a while to catch up, but she's now a lovely mare and very exciting for the future. She's an unbelievable cross-country horse – very obedient in her mouth, quick and brave, and as she's got older she's learnt to control her power and the dressage has become easier.

She was fourth at Saumur and placed in an advanced class at Gatcombe and at Blenheim as an eight-year-old – and seventh in her first four-star at Kentucky the next year. For a nine-year-old mare, that was pretty smart. She's always showjumped well after cross-country, which is a great help.

I went to Luhmühlen feeling she had a very good chance – she'd won an advanced class at Chatsworth on her previous run. The first water complex here comes up

early and has a history of catching horses out. It might be something optical – it seems to jump differently at different times of the day. I'd thought we'd met it well and had got up in the air, but the next moment we were both submerged, headfirst. Qwanza was absolutely fine and won on her next run, at Aston-le-Walls. She's had a bit of time off since through injury, but is on her way back.

I've had several of her full- and half-sisters: Sintra BK, who I competed to three-star and then sold to the American rider, Jules Stiller; Paul Ridgeon's Urma BK, a seven-year-old mare I'm riding at two-star level now, and eight-year-old Teseo, who won an advanced on his last run in 2013 and is part-owned with my father-in-law, Philip Channer. Their dam, Kurda 66, is a plain, rather blocky mare with 'a leg at each corner' and her offspring aren't classically beautiful, but they are as tough and competitive as you could wish for.

QUIMBO, MR CRUISE CONTROL, NEREO AND AVEBURY

Westwood Stud, 2013

HERE ARE MY FOUR CCI**** WINNERS, Quimbo, Mr Cruise Control, Nereo and Avebury, taken for a *Horse & Hound* feature. You can see that they are all different shapes, but what's more interesting is how much more different they are to each other when they're not eventing fit. Then, Quimbo looks the most thoroughbred of the quartet, even though he probably has the least thoroughbred in him; Mr Cruise Control looks like a gigantic hunter; Nereo stays reasonably elegant, while in the middle of the winter Avebury looks like a hairy kid's pony. It shows how you can change the shape of a horse with work – and how quickly they revert back without work.

AVEBURY

Gatcombe, 2013

THIS WAS A RATHER HAIRY DAY. First, I managed to tip Quimbo up on the cross-country at Gatcombe and felt like I'd bust my ribs. I rode Teseo and Tilikum in the intermediate championship next morning and Tilikum had pulled pretty hard, so I was fairly uncomfortable by the time the Open Championship got underway.

I rode Avebury first, trying to do as little as possible on top to minimise the pain. We jumped into the water, and turned just too quickly to the fence in the water. I realised the end of the jump had a fixed pole on it, and as the horse took off, I thought his shoulder was going to hit it. I put a hand on the pole to push it off and my knee hit it hard, which dragged me backwards out of the saddle. Avebury kept going and I pulled myself back into the plate, but now I had sore ribs and a sore knee.

Then it was Nereo's turn. He lost a shoe early on in the course and was skidding around. Again, I was attempting to sit pretty still because of the pain. We turned too tightly into the fence into the water and it felt like he started to slip, and he stopped, for only about the second time in his whole career.

CALICO JOE, AVEBURY AND NEREO

Burghley, 2013

I DIDN'T HAVE ANY BURNING DESIRE TO RIDE three horses at Burghley – it just happened that when the organisers were a little short of entries, they rang me and asked if I wanted to take three, and I couldn't see why not. Yes, cross-country day was busy, but I'm not good at sitting round for hours watching other riders anyway.

I rode Calico Joe (left) first, and when he whipped round inside the time so easily I think some people fell into the trap of thinking the time was more achievable than it was. They don't realise how quick he is – he doesn't get tired, doesn't pull and is very economical. It was a proper Burghley track and I was surprised how easy he made it feel, particularly the second half. He was seven seconds under the time and it could have been 15 if I'd pushed him.

Avebury (below) jumped a perfect round and also got the time, but Nereo (overleaf) was a couple of seconds over.

He finds Burghley very hard work; the little hillocks and undulations feel much greater than they are underneath his huge stride. All three were in the top ten after cross-country: Avebury was second behind Jock Paget, Nereo was fourth and Calico Joe seventh.

Calico Joe clattered his way round the showjumping with four down, but the other two just had one fence down apiece, which was pretty good on a day when there were hardly any clear rounds. Nereo's rail was entirely my fault – I changed my mind about what stride we should be on – but Avebury's was a little naughty.

I knew Jock would win as his horse Clifton Promise is a very good jumper and he had a rail in hand. My three were second, third and eighth and I won the HSBC FEI Classics series, which gives a big cash bonus for the rider who gets the most points at the four-star events in the past year.

However, Burghley 2013 didn't end there. When I was driving to Le Lion d'Angers the following month, my federation rang me to say that Jock's horse had tested positive for a banned substance, reserpine, at Burghley, and to prepare myself for the media onslaught. I dealt with all that, but the next morning Wiggy rang to say that three people we know who have nothing to do with horses had been on the phone because there was a picture of me on Nereo in *TheDaily Telegraph* with a headline that ran something like "Champion fails drugs test", alongside a picture of me instead of Jock, and that's not an implication you want splashed around the press. I was very angry with the paper.

I couldn't see any way that Jock could keep his title, and this meant that Avebury would become the first horse in Burghley's 52-year history to win it back to back. But it took until May for him officially to be

announced the winner, and the handling of the whole thing and the timing of the announcement was appalling.

I was in Kentucky with Avebury when the news came through, on the day of the first horse inspection. It was too late for any publicity about the fact that we were there attempting to win the second leg of the Grand Slam, which I thought was very hard on the event and on Rolex, the Grand Slam sponsor.

I landed myself in a bit of hot water over an interview I did on the subject. A New Zealand journalist, who owns a share in one of Jock's horses, kept asking me to talk about how good it was of Jock to "gift" (as he put it) me Burghley. I gave him two perfectly clean versions, but the third one did contain quite a bit of swearing, and it was obviously the one he used. It was apparently on prime time television news in New Zealand!

JET SET IV

Le Lion d'Angers, 2013

JET SET IV WAS BRED BY LUIS ÀLVAREZ DE CERVERA, who showjumped his sire, Nordico, at championship level, and he's out of an Argentinian thoroughbred mare.

I first saw Jet Set as a just-broken three-year-old on Luis's farm. I had a ride on him and really liked him, but Luis wanted a lot of money for him so I suggested he showjumped him. Luis was living the dream as a breeder and I knew I'd get a chance to get the horse more cheaply once he hadn't made it as a top-class jumper!

Luis and his son Eduardo jumped him – he got to finals of the Spanish Sunshine Tour as a five-year-old, jumping 1m 35cm – but Luis kept telling me to come and try him again, so when I was over in October 2012, I did. He had changed sales tactics by then and had spent a couple of months telling Wiggy that Jet Set would be perfect for her to ride... We got there and Wiggy had a sit on him, but at 17hh he was far too big for her. I ended up buying him, and paying much more than I'd planned!

When I got him home and galloped him, he was unbelievable. I worked him all that winter, and when I took him cross-country schooling he was just like Luis had said – he wanted to jump everything, not because he was wild and excited, but because he wanted to please you so much.

In the beginning he had quite a lot of knee action, but he quickly learnt to take a longer stride and adopt a slower rhythm. The moment you sit on him, you know he's in a different league.

He had a run-out at his first event, but that didn't matter – he felt every bit as good as I thought he would. He whizzed through novice level, and Libby Sellar bought him as he was turning intermediate. Her daughter Charlie, who plays polo, came to look at him with her, and she had a sit on him. I had a hard time getting her off him; he's like that, he switches to suit whoever is on him because he wants to please so much.

In this picture, he's finishing second in the Young Horse World Championships for six-year-olds at Le Lion d'Angers. In my view, a lot of the young horses who do well there aren't necessarily going to be four-star horses. They tend to be early-maturing types who look very elegant in the dressage, whereas often really good horses look rangy and a bit weak as six- and seven-year-olds, and then mature later. Jet Set is big and leggy, and for him to come second at Le Lion is quite something, I think. He won 110 points in on his first season of competition in 2013, which is an extraordinary feat.

QUIMBO

Badminton, 2014

THIS PICTURE OF QUIMBO giving the famous Vicarage Vee fence a foot of air makes it look as if Badminton 2014 might have been a success for me. Instead it was a disastrous weekend. I took two former four-star winners there and thought I had a definite chance of winning it for the first time after 30 years of trying.

I did realise, however, when it rained so much that it wouldn't suit Quimbo; when it's wet he jumps very high, which is a great feeling if you are on top, but not ideal when you've got to go across country for four miles. It doesn't feel like he's frightened or anything, he just gets far too high in the air, as if he's showing you what he can do.

He felt fantastic as far as the Outlander Bank. There, because he was jumping so big, I tried to angle the jump up the bank so he could see the skinny brush that was the third element of it when he jumped through the keyhole on top of the bank. Quimbo can be a bit tricky if he jumps very big and hasn't seen exactly what he has to jump at the end of a combination. However, I got too much angle and he ended up facing the solid part of the side of the keyhole, and refused.

I thought I'd jump a couple more fences before pulling him up and taking him to another event, as it wasn't as though he needs the experience. But seeing as I was then at the furthest point of the course, I thought I'd jump round to the Stickpile, which was the fence nearest the stables!

After that, I was really looking forward to riding Nereo. He was equal seventh after dressage, and in those conditions when no one was getting close to the optimum time because of the wind and mud, we had an excellent chance. I know him very well, and he's a hardened campaigner who knows how to dig deep when he gets a little tired.

He warmed up beautifully and we set off. It felt perfect – until the Gatehouse New Pond at fence 14. I still don't know why he left a front leg at the rail coming out of the water. I had no idea this was coming and I tipped off the front end. For sure I should have stayed on him – but I didn't. Perhaps it was because it had felt so effortless – we hadn't made the hint of a mistake anywhere, which is unusual at this level – and it was therefore so unexpected.

It's also possible that there had been had been an error with the frangible pin, a safety device used to hold upright fences together. I came into the rails into the water on a sharper line than other riders had – most had jumped further to the left. Like many experienced cross-country horses, Nereo often "sits" his hindlegs on a fence into water as a way of braking and balancing himself. When we landed in the water it felt as if our normal braking system hadn't quite worked and, for some reason, he wanted to shoot forward through the water much faster than usual, which could be why he left that foreleg on the way out.

It wasn't until I was picking myself up off the ground that I heard that the pin in the first part of the complex had broken, which would have made the top rail collapse underneath Nereo. When I said to an official "I didn't think he hit it that hard", he said: "No, you didn't – we'd just rested the rail on top of the post".

Had they removed the pin to use elsewhere because so many were broken that day? Nereo is very sensitive and suspicious of anything that isn't how he expects it to be and the fence not acting in its usual way when he brushed it would have unsettled him and made him go faster. Ultimately, though, I shouldn't have fallen off, and that's that.

AVEBURY

Barbury Castle, 2014

HERE'S AVEBURY, BACK ON FORM AT BARBURY after a disappointing run at Kentucky CCI**** in the spring. He never felt himself in the States, but maybe some horses have a real sense of 'place' because he felt delighted to be at Barbury. It's a lovely event just a couple of miles away from home, and Avebury has now won the main CIC*** class there three years in a row. There can't be many – if any – horses to have done that at international level.

He was well ahead of a huge field after the dressage, showjumped clear – as he has on each of the occasions on which he has won there – and by the time I set off across country I knew I had plenty of

time in hand and could afford a few time-faults. I never had to put him under any pressure and he had his ears pricked the whole way. This picture shows us jumping the Combine Harvester fence three from the finish, which looked very dramatic in the wide-open spaces and rolling downland of Barbury Castle.

Lily and Zach came with us, and the second picture shows the three of us with the Barbury trophy. Now I've won it three times, do I get to keep it?!

ANNABEL SCRIMGEOUR

Westwood Stud, 2014

WORKING WITH ANNABEL SCRIMGEOUR in the past few years has definitely helped my flatwork. I've known her for a long time – she used to go to Mark Todd's and help ride some of his, and then she got involved with Henrietta Knight's National Hunt yard. She's also a top-level judge and trains a lot of people.

When Avebury was at two-star level, I bumped into her and asked if she'd give me some lessons, and also if she'd come and ride some horses for me. I'm probably not the ideal pupil as I have to be in the right frame of mind for dressage lessons, and I'm not used to having someone tell me what to do every day.

But Annabel and I work well together, and when Henrietta gave up training, she started coming up here most days. She usually rides four horses, and sometimes gallops some as well as riding in the school. Some days she gives me lessons, and she even helps puts jumps up and down for me. She likes watching when I am working with Luis Àlvarez de Cervera, and takes things away from those sessions that she can use to help the horses on the flat.

When I go to any other trainers, Annabel comes and watches, so she can then help me work on things they might suggest. I feel she has made a big difference and that the horses are going better all the time.

JET SET IV
Westwood Stud, 2014

HERE, I'M WORKING JET SET in my outdoor school at home. Mirrors in the school are one of the best investments you can make, although it took me a long time to realise that. You can see instantly what's happening underneath you; they don't argue or answer back, and when I'm in a real strop they don't get upset!

I think Jet Set could be the best horse I've had. He's a beautiful jumper, incredibly rideable, a superb galloper and lovely on the flat. He's very exciting – and could be my Rio Olympics horse in 2016. I've also got his full-brother, Liberto II, who is now five and owned by Nicky Salmon.

TILIKUM

Westwood Stud, 2014

THIS IS TILIKUM, who was also bred by Ana Beca and is owned by Libby Sellar. He's eight now and did his first three-star in the spring of 2014 at Belton. I think he'll be very smart – he's a great jumper and, although quite strong in his mouth at the moment, he's getting better.

He went well at his two two-star three-day-events last year, Tattersalls and Le Lion d'Angers, but I think he'll be a horse who comes into himself in a couple of years' time. He's not as straightforward as some of them – he has problems controlling his own power – and Rio might come a bit soon for him, but he'll be on the list of potentials.

I'd expect Teseo, who's the same age and out of the same mare as Qwanza, to be ahead of him, though. He's by a thoroughbred and is very classy – he won an advanced class in 2013 as a seven-year-old. He can be a bit lively in the dressage at the moment, which seems to be a trait from that dam.

LILY
AND ZACH
NICHOLSON

Westwood Stud, 2014

I'VE LEARNT THAT IT'S IMPORTANT for children to have good ponies. Lily and Zach have superb ones, Tyson and Smartie, and it's much more fun for them than it was for Melissa and Rebecca.

Lily, who was born in March 2005, is a proper girl who wants to learn and for her pony to go well; Zach, who was born in February 2009, just wants to gallop everywhere. He'll be like I was at Pony Club and I don't envy his instructor!

It's fun for me to see them enjoying their ponies, though, and because they don't come to many events with us, they get excited when they do because it's a special occasion, rather than the chore it probably became for Melissa and Rebecca.

Sport is a great thing for kids. I'd encourage them to do something else as a job if they could, but I could hardly say no if they wanted to take it up full-time, and would just try and make sure that they have nice horses to ride and that they enjoy it.